7/98   15. 00

THOMAS MERTON

Poet, Prophet, Priest

Jennifer Fisher Bryant

Eerdmans Books for Young Readers
Grand Rapids, Michigan / Cambridge, U.K.

© 1997 Wm. B. Eerdmans Publishing Co.
Published 1997 by
Eerdmans Books for Young Readers
an imprint of
Wm. B. Eerdmans Publishing Co.
255 Jefferson Ave. S.E., Grand Rapids, Michigan 49503 /
P.O. Box 163, Cambridge CB3 9PU U.K.

Printed in the United States of America

02 01 00 99 98 97   7 6 5 4 3 2 1

Library of Congress Cataloging-in-Publication Data

Bryant, Jennifer.
Thomas Merton: poet, prophet, priest / by Jennifer Bryant.
p.   cm.
Summary: Traces the life of the Trappist monk who became one of
America's best-known spiritual writers, describing his childhood and
worldly education, his faith journey, his writing career, and his involvement
in social issues of his time.
ISBN 0-8028-5109-6 (cloth: alk. paper) —
ISBN 0-8028-5140-1 (pbk.: alk. paper)
1. Merton, Thomas, 1915-1968 — Juvenile literature. 2. Trappists —
United States — Biography — Juvenile literature.
[1. Merton, Thomas, 1915-1968. 2. Monks. 3. Authors, American.]
I. Title.
BX4705.M542B78   1997
271′.12502
[B] — DC20   96-2783
CIP
AC

The author and publisher gratefully acknowledge permission
to quote the materials listed on pages 201-2.

For Leigh and Neil,
Les and June,
with love and gratitude
for your encouragement and support

Contents

1. Ordination   1

2. Beginnings   8

3. Where Is Home?   17

4. European Roots   28

5. Escape to England   38

6. A Searching Time   52

7. The Reluctant Christian   66

8. Home, at Last   83

9. Inside the Walls   106

10. The Writing Monk of Gethsemani   126

11. Seeds of Change   141

12. A Different View   158

13. Final Journey   175

My Sources for This Book	193
Suggestions for Further Reading	195
Selected Bibliography	199
Acknowledgments	201
Index	203

CHAPTER 1

Ordination

O n the night of May 25, 1949, Thomas Merton could not sleep. He tossed and turned on a straw mattress in his cell at the Abbey of Gethsemani, the Trappist monastery near Bardstown, Kentucky. All through the week, the anticipation had built up inside of him until he felt he might explode from nervous tension. "In three days, if I am alive and if the Archbishop does not fall down and break his leg, I should be a priest," he wrote in his journal on May 23. "I keep thinking: 'I shall say Mass — I shall say Mass.'"

For Tom, priestly ordination was truly a miracle — positive proof of God's grace and forgiveness. Before joining the Trappists, he had wandered through much of his young life in a chaotic, self-centered fashion. He had spent his teenage years in Europe, attending prominent boarding schools and traveling widely in his spare time. Intelligent and fun-loving, he had a gift for writing and harbored ambitions of becoming a novelist.

During his freshman year at England's Cambridge University, however, he ignored his studies in favor of pursuits he found more pleasurable: drinking, attending parties, and dating women. From time to time, he had the gnawing feeling that something was missing, that life held some deeper purpose than self-gratification. Nevertheless, he avoided religious commitment and continued to live a selfish, day-to-day existence. Then the news that one of his girlfriends was pregnant suddenly forced him to consider the consequences of his delinquent behavior. He went to America to live with his grandparents and to make a fresh start.

It was there, while attending New York's Columbia University, that Tom was baptized as a Catholic at Corpus Christi Church. When the date for his baptism was set, Tom remembered, "I walked out of the rectory that evening happier and more contented than I had ever been in my life." He described his baptism as "[a] beginning, and a most generous one, on the part of God."

A zealous convert, Tom attended daily Mass, disciplined himself in private prayer, and read widely on the history and philosophy of the Christian faith. When he was twenty-six, he made his first retreat to the Abbey of Gethsemani, an event which proved to be a turning point in his life. There was a suggestion of just how transformative this event would be in his journal entry from about three weeks before. He was in the library doing research on the Trappists when he was struck by the simple beauty and spiritual clarity of the monk's life:

What wonderful happiness there was, then, in the world! There were still men on this miserable, noisy, cruel earth, who tasted the marvelous joy of silence and solitude, who dwelt in . . . secluded monasteries, where the news and desires and appetites and conflicts of the world no longer reached them. . . . Their clear vision, clean of the world's smoke . . . [was] raised to heaven. . . . They were poor, they had nothing, and therefore they were free and possessed everything. . . . Everything around them was simple and primitive and poor, because they were the least and the last of men, they had made themselves outcasts. . . . Above all, they had found Christ.

In December of 1941, he made a second retreat to the Kentucky monastery. This time he shocked everyone by deciding to stay for good. "I think most of us at Oakham and Cambridge were very surprised that he should have become a Trappist monk," said John Barber, one of Tom's English schoolmates. "He was always, at school, kicking over the traces." On the other hand, Barber commented, "We realized that he had the intellectual ability to do whatever he took up, to perfection almost, and he did just that. He had the innate capability of that type of dedicated life." Perhaps the only person who was not surprised was Tom's best friend, Robert Lax. "I think he was just looking for a direction in life," Lax explained. "I think that he felt blocked at one point or another in the choices that were offered him, say, by the university or by the world or anything else, and that if he was drawn to the monastery, it was because he could see a kind of freedom there — paradoxical — but a kind of freedom in which he could grow and become fully the thing that he must have felt he was potentially. And so what he was after was to become himself."

In joining the Cistercians of the Strict Observance — or Trappists — Tom became a member of one of the most conservative religious communities in the United States. He became "Father Louis," and took vows of poverty, chastity, obedience, and silence (Trappists communicate through sign language). In those early days at Gethsemani, there was minimal contact with the outside world: no newspapers, magazines, radios, or TVs were permitted, and written correspondence was strictly limited. The daily routine was a simple one, consisting mainly of prayer, meditation, and manual labor.

This austere and regimented lifestyle contrasted sharply with the way Tom had lived before. But in submitting to the external limitations of monastery life, he found that his internal life flourished. "[There is] an innocence and liberty of soul that come to those who have thrown away all preoccupation with themselves and their own ideas and judgements and opinions and desires, and are perfectly content to take things as they come to them from the hands of God and through the wishes and commands of their superiors," he wrote in his autobiography.

That autobiography is *The Seven Storey Mountain,* and Abbot Dom Frederic, the head of the monastery, played a role in its development. He recognized that Tom was a gifted writer, so he arranged for Tom to undertake a variety of writing projects for the monastery. He also encouraged Tom to write his autobiography as a way to help him understand his past. Tom's life story became a substantial manuscript that was published in 1948 and — much to everyone's surprise — quickly became a best-seller. This put Tom in the awkward position of being a popular and sought-after author confined to a silent, remote monastery. Such fame was unexpected and set him apart from the rest of his order: "When a man becomes 'an author' in the world outside, he adapts himself comfortably to the situation by imitating the other authors he meets at parties," Tom observed in his journal. "[But] an author in a Trappist monastery is like a duck in a chicken coop. And he would give anything in the world to be a chicken instead of a duck."

Despite his mixed feelings about the writing life, Tom went on to publish more than fifty books, as well as dozens of essays, poems, and articles. *The Seven Storey Mountain,* however, remained his best-known and most influential book. In the first year after its publication, it had sold over 100,000 copies.

In May of 1949, eight years after joining the monastery, Tom was ordained as a priest. His editor, Robert Giroux, who had been friends with Merton since his days at Columbia, attended the ordination ceremonies.

Like many of Tom's former classmates, Giroux had been surprised when Tom had joined the Trappists. But during his three-day visit, he began to understand why Tom had been attracted to Gethsemani: "The abbey was a new experience for me," Giroux recalled. "I was impressed by the simplicity of the place. All the monks were very direct, and their reactions were simple and open. It was a happy place, and a very hard-working place. . . . Far from the perfect peace and quiet you expected, you heard the rattle of farm machinery all day. The serenity was interior. [The monks] sang songs at intervals all day long, starting at two in the morning . . . when their day began. They retired at sunset — a healthy farmer's life."

Tom's priestly ordination included three days of church services, vows, rituals, and anointing. In the quiet hours before the first ceremony began, Tom reflected on his earlier life. "I was afraid that the whole Church might come down on my head, because of what I used to be," he wrote in his journal. "I have done all things badly. I have thrown away great opportunities. [But] my infidelity to Christ, instead of making me sick with despair, drives me to throw myself all the more blindly into the arms of His mercy."

To his friends, however, it was clear that Tom had undergone a remarkable spiritual transformation and had indeed left his old ways behind. "In the pictures of Merton's ordination day," Robert Lax recalled, ". . . he looks much younger than he did in his college pictures, or in anything leading up to that. . . . He does look as though he had been reborn and very young. . . . He was very happy at this time."

This ordination was indeed a milestone in what would become one of the most intriguing spiritual journeys of modern times. For Tom, it was a profound and powerful event that marked his commitment to a new life, a new path. "My priestly ordination was, I felt, the one great secret for which I had been born," he later wrote. And for millions of others as well, who would come to know Thomas Merton through his writings, it was a journey that was just beginning.

CHAPTER 2

Beginnings

Thomas Feverel Merton was born in Prades, France, on January 31, 1915. As World War I raged on into its second year, the battlefield spread over the once-peaceful countryside of southern France. "In a year of a great war, and down in the shadow of some French mountains on the borders of Spain, I came into the world," Merton wrote in his autobiography *The Seven Storey Mountain*. "Not many hundreds of miles away from the house where I was born, they were picking up the men who rotted in the rainy ditches among the dead horses . . . in a forest of trees without branches along the river Marne."

His father, Owen Merton, was a professional artist who had spent his childhood days in New Zealand. "Once, when one of the Antarctic expeditions came that way, my father nearly joined it," Tom wrote. "[He] had a lot of energy and independence." At first, young Owen had difficulty convincing his family to let him go to

Europe to study art, but he eventually succeeded. It was there, in Paris, that Owen met an American artist, Ruth Jenkins, who later became his wife.

The newly married couple moved to Prades in south-western France, where they hoped to lead a simple life, painting and raising a family. When Tom was born, he was named after his godfather, Tom Bennett, an English doctor who was a good friend of Owen Merton's. Tom writes that his baptism "was almost certainly Father's idea, because he had grown up with a deep and well-developed faith, according to the doctrines of the Church of England." Ruth Merton, on the other hand, "attached not too much importance" to formal religion.

Tom's mother watched his development that first year with intense interest. Throughout Tom's infancy and early childhood, she kept a diary in which she took recorded details of his physical, emotional, and intellectual development. She noted his preferences for certain foods (oatmeal), activities (talking and running), and objects (the gas-light on the stove). Years later, upon reading these early diary entries, Merton wrote, "I was nobody's dream-child. [My mother's diary] reflects some astonishment at the stubborn and seemingly spontaneous development of completely unpredictable features in my character, things she had never bargained for."

Although the Mertons had hoped to make France their home, their stay in Prades was short-lived. The war was a constant threat, and though the fighting seemed far enough away, France no longer seemed a safe place to raise a family. When Tom was just a year old, his parents packed up their belongings, took the train to the western coast, and boarded an ocean liner bound for the United States.

Ruth's parents met them in the port of New York and took them to their home in the nearby suburb of Douglaston. Tom soon discovered that "Pop" and "Bonnemaman" (French slang for "grandmother") had very different personalities. "Pop was a buoyant and excitable man," Tom wrote, "who, on docks, boats, trains, in stations, in elevators, on busses, in hotels, in restaurants, used to get keyed up and start ordering everybody around, and making new arrangements, and changing them on the spur of the moment. My grandmother . . . was just the opposite, and her natural deliberateness and hesitancy and hatred of activity always seemed to increase in proportion to Pop's excesses."

Sharing the Jenkinses' home was a delightful experience for young Tom, but proved stressful for his parents. A few months later, the couple rented a house in Flushing, Long Island, where they regained some of the privacy they had enjoyed in Europe. The house itself was "very old and rickety," but Tom's parents were willing to tolerate less-than-perfect conditions if it meant a return to independent living.

The Mertons settled into a peaceful routine that had eluded them in war-torn France. Owen plunged into his painting with renewed vigor, producing enough watercolors to warrant an exhibition at a cooperative gallery in Flushing. But he didn't earn enough money from selling his paintings, so he worked as a landscape gardener for several rich families in the neighborhood. "He was a very good gardener," Tom recalled. "[He] understood flowers, and knew how to make things grow. What is more, he liked this kind of work almost as much as painting."

It was from his father that Tom gained an appreciation for natural beauty and landscapes. He also shared his father's ability to observe life with a certain amount of detachment. This trait was necessary for Owen's career as a painter and landscaper, and later served Tom in his vocation as writer. Indeed, throughout his lifetime, Tom drew upon his creative heritage as a source of identity. He was obviously proud that his parents were artists: at the beginning of *The Seven Storey Mountain,* he wrote, "They were in the world and not of it, not because they were saints, but in a different way: because they were artists. The integrity of an artist lifts a man above the level of the world without delivering him from it."

In November of 1918, Tom's brother, John Paul, was born. He was much calmer than Tom by nature, and Tom wrote that everyone was impressed by "his constant and unruffled happiness." Tom, now nearly three years old, had firmly established his place in the family and was not threatened by the tiny addition.

Still, he longed for a companion his own age with whom he could play during the long afternoons when his parents were busy painting. When he discovered that John Paul's interests were limited to eating and sleeping, Tom created an imaginary friend named Jack who had an imaginary dog named Doolittle. Tom's parents encouraged his imaginary play, even though the presence of these "friends" occasionally produced unexpected problems for his mother. "Once I went shopping with her," Tom remembered, "and refused to cross Main Street, Flushing, for fear that the imaginary dog, Doolittle, might get run over by real cars."

As Tom approached the age of five, Ruth Merton sent away for a home-schooling kit. Using its tools, she began to teach Tom the basics of reading, writing, and geography. Ruth's standards were high, and when Tom didn't measure up to her expectations, he was punished. "One night," he recalled, "I was sent to bed early for stubbornly spelling 'which' without the first 'h': 'w-i-c-h.' I remember brooding about this as an injustice. . . . After all, I was still only five years old."

While spelling remained a bit of a struggle for Tom, the study of geography became a favorite pastime. Maps and charts of the continents and oceans stirred Tom's already active imagination, suggesting the possibility of travel and discovery. As he learned more about distant lands and their inhabitants, Tom realized that the world extended far beyond his own rural American community. In his free time, he began drawing pictures of boats, "ocean liners with many funnels and hundreds of portholes, and waves all around as jagged as a saw, and the air full of 'v's' for the sea-gulls." He later observed that he was obviously eager "for [some] kind of footloose life."

Although Tom was frequently stubborn and had a growing tendency to daydream, his intellect thrived under Ruth's strict tutelage. But his parents gave him little religious education; the family never went to church in Flushing. "The only explanation I have," Tom wrote, "is the guess that Mother must have had strong views on the subject." Yet Ruth Merton frequently attended a nearby Quaker Meeting, where the deep, meditative silences were only occasionally interrupted by a member's brief prayer or address. "This was the only kind of religion for which she had any use," Tom commented.

Nevertheless, young Tom manifested an intense interest in religious prayers, symbols, and traditions. When his father's mother, who was from New Zealand, visited briefly in 1919, she taught him the words to the Lord's Prayer. It made a profound impression on him. "After that," he wrote in *The Seven Storey Mountain*, "I did not forget it, even though I went for years without saying it at all."

Not long afterward, Owen Merton took a job as an organist at a nearby Episcopal church. Tom was only too glad to accompany his father to the Sunday services, where he sat quietly in the front pew and observed the

Christian rituals. With an artist's objectivity, he studied every visual detail of the church: the altar candles, the glorious choir, the intricate stained-glass windows, the worn hymnals, and the adjacent overgrown graveyard. But because he was there more as an observer than a participant, Tom remained ignorant of the meaning behind Christian liturgies, hymns, and rituals. "One came out of the church with a kind of comfortable and satisfied feeling that something had been done that needed to be done, and that was all I knew about it."

His father's sudden employment as an organist (a job he disliked) puzzled Tom at first, but gradually the reason became clear: Ruth Merton was very ill with cancer, and the family needed extra money. At her request, the origin and details of her sickness were not discussed with the children, for fear that it would make them "morbid." When she entered the hospital for treatment, Tom and John Paul moved back into their grandparents' house in Douglaston. "I did not weep when I was not allowed to go and see [Mother]," Merton wrote. "I was content to run in the woods with the dogs, or climb trees, or pester the chickens, or play around in the clean little studio where Bonnemaman sometimes painted china."

Tom's apparent indifference to his mother's tragic situation was no doubt his only defense against natural feelings of attachment to her. The fact that no one explained the nature of illness, death, or grief to him probably compounded his bewilderment, for he must have sensed that a great loss was imminent.

When at last he did hear from his mother, she was gravely ill. In his autobiography, he recalls how sadness overwhelmed him when his true feelings surfaced:

> One day Father gave me a note to read. I was very surprised. . . . It was in my mother's handwriting. . . . [She] was informing me, by mail, that she was about to die, and would never see me again.
>
> I took the note out under the maple tree in the back yard. . . . A tremendous weight of sadness and depression settled on me. It was not the grief of a child, with pangs of sorrow and many tears. It had something of the heavy perplexity and gloom of adult grief, and was therefore all the more of a burden because it was, to that extent, unnatural.

Lacking any spiritual context in which to place his mother's death, six-year-old Tom was forced to try to make some sense of the crisis himself. "It was not until I became a Catholic, 20 years later, that it finally occurred to me to pray for my mother," he said.

Ruth's death seemed like a cruel, arbitrary act of fate, and to a young and sensitive child, this randomness must have been terrifying. For the first five years of his life, his mother had looked after him, cared for him, played with him, and instructed him. Then, quite suddenly, she was gone, never to return. Under these circumstances, it would be natural for Tom to wonder how many other loved ones he might lose in this way. This fear of abandonment produced a feeling of insecurity that plagued him throughout most of his youth. It would not be until he entered the Abbey of Gethsemani — about twenty-one years later — that he would once again feel truly at peace.

CHAPTER 3

Where Is Home?

Ruth Merton's death signaled the beginning of many changes for young Tom. Tom's memory of the day his mother died — October 3, 1921 — is vivid: "Father went into a room alone, and I followed him and found him weeping, over by the window." Tom wrote. "He must have thought of the days before the war, when he had first met Mother in Paris, when she had been so happy, . . . and had danced, and had been full of ideas and plans and ambitions for herself and for him and for their children. It had not turned out as they had planned. And now it was all over." Soon after the funeral, Tom's grief-stricken father left New York in search of new places to paint. By plunging himself immediately into work, Owen Merton hoped to escape the overwhelming sadness he felt.

While their father traveled, Tom and his younger brother continued to live with their grandparents, Martha and Samuel Jenkins, in Douglaston. Tom was enrolled in first grade at the local public school. After a few weeks, however, it was apparent that he needed more of a challenge, and he was moved up to second grade. Despite this "promotion," he remained sad and confused about his mother's death, and he missed his father. Unfortunately, the school's atmosphere did little to cheer him up. "[It was an] evil-smelling grey annex on top of the hill," he wrote in his autobiography.

Owen Merton returned in the spring of 1922, announcing that he had found a suitable place to paint. Tom was flattered when his father asked him to come along, because it meant that his father respected his maturity: "Mother's death had made one thing evident," he wrote in *The Seven Storey Mountain*. "Father . . . was not tied down to any one place. He could go wherever he needed to go, to find subjects and get ideas, and I was old enough to go with him." John Paul, who was too young to spend several hours a day without adult supervision, stayed behind with his grandparents.

As soon as the school year was over, Tom and his father traveled by boat and train to Provincetown on Cape Cod (the easternmost peninsula of Massachusetts). Provincetown was a well-established artists' colony whose peaceful seaside landscape attracted many American painters. Tom's initial impression of the town was that it "smelled of dead fish," but he soon discovered an activity that kept him occupied for most of the summer: "There were countless fishing boats, of all sizes, tied up along the wharves; and you could run all day on the decks of the schooners, and no one would prevent you, or chase you away."

Tom also discovered that his father, unlike his mother, had few rules regarding behavior. He remembered feeling "almost completely overwhelmed with surprise and awe" when his father bought him a chocolate bar on the train to Provincetown and allowed him to eat the entire thing. "Before," Tom wrote, "candy had always been strictly rationed." His father scolded him only once the entire summer, when he "refused to eat an orange."

As his father painted the Cape Cod landscape, Tom also took an interest in the details of the land, water, and sky around him. Like his father, he had an acute visual memory and a genuine appreciation for natural beauty: "That summer was full of low sand dunes, and coarse grasses as sharp as wires, growing from the white sand," he wrote in *The Seven Storey Mountain*. "I saw the breakers of the grey sea come marching in towards the land, and I looked out at the ocean. Geography had begun to become a reality." Tom's ability to remember particular features of places where he lived and traveled was something he drew upon throughout his lifetime. Later, when he became a writer, he exercised this talent frequently, using it to recall and create scenes and backgrounds for his novels, poems, and memoirs.

At the end of the summer, father and son returned to Douglaston, where Tom was re-enrolled in public school. Owen Merton set off in search of new artistic subjects, then returned a few weeks later to retrieve his older son. Would Tom be interested in going with him to Bermuda? he asked.

Their ship left New York the following week and, after three days' travel, dropped anchor in the crystal blue-green waters surrounding Bermuda. In 1922, this small Atlantic island was not the vacation paradise it is today. "It was simply a curious island," Tom wrote, "where the British had a naval base and where there were no automobiles and not much of anything else either."

When Tom and his father arrived, they went directly to the boarding house where the two agreed Tom would stay during the week. (His father had chosen it because it was close to the island's only school.) Because there were no other children around, the British officers who sat on the porch "and smoked their pipes and talked, if they talked at all, about matters extemely profane" would be Tom's only companions. Meanwhile, Tom's father accepted an invitation to stay with friends, "literary people and artists," nearby in Somerset, presumably to reduce expenses.

Had Tom's mother been alive, she would certainly not have approved. But the more lenient Owen Merton, torn between his personal and professional commitments, was willing to give these arrangements a try. "It must have been very difficult for Father to try to make all these decisions," Tom wrote. "He wanted me to go to school, and he wanted me to be with him. When both these things ceased to be possible at the same time, he first decided in favor of the school."

For the next few weeks, Tom went to the island school, where he struggled to learn multiplication and long division. His father, meanwhile, painted landscapes, working hard to improve his craft. Then one day he appeared at the boarding house and told Tom to pack his bags. His father had been forced to "reconsider" his original decision, Tom wrote, "[because of] the nature of the place where I had to live, and the kind of talk I heard there, all day long, with my wide-open . . . understanding."

Tom's father took him out of school and brought Tom to the house where he was living with some friends. Once again, Tom adjusted quickly to the new situation. In his autobiography, he shares his thoughts about the unpredictable nature of his early childhood:

> It is almost impossible to make much sense out of the continual rearrangement of our lives and our plans from month to month. . . . Yet every new development came to me as a reasonable and worthy change. Sometimes I had to go to school, sometimes I did not. Sometimes Father and I were living together, sometimes I was with strangers and only saw him from time to time. People came into our lives and went out of our lives. We had now one set of friends, now another. Things were always changing. I accepted it all. Why should it ever have occurred to me that nobody else lived like that? To me, it seemed as natural as the variations of the weather and the seasons.

Owen Merton's artistic output was prodigious during the next several months. He produced dozens of fine watercolors depicting the lush Bermudian landscape, the small, colorful island homes, and the shimmering blue ocean. He gained confidence in his work, and he accepted an invitation to participate in a major New York exhibition to be held later that year.

While his father put the finishing touches on his paintings and prepared them for shipment, Tom explored the nearby beaches, played in the sand, and climbed the magnificent rocks where he could stand and look out over the wide blue ocean. He was relieved to be free of multiplication and long division, but he feared that his former teacher might force him to return to school: "[She] passed along that road [near the place Tom and his father were staying] on her bicycle on her way home," Tom recalled, "and if I was playing by the road, I had to get out of sight for fear that she would send the truant officer around and make me come back."

Toward the end of the summer of 1923, Owen left to attend the exhibition in New York, leaving Tom in the care of his friends in Somerset. The exhibition was a success, and Tom's father used some of the money he earned to pay his son's passage back to New York. But no sooner had Tom returned than he was faced with another major change: "Father was going to sail to France, with his friends, and leave me in America," Tom wrote.

And so for the third time since his mother's death, Tom was left in the care of his grandparents, whose predictable, middle-class lifestyle was very different from the bohemian wanderings to which Tom had grown accustomed. Each day after a hot, hearty breakfast, "Pop" went to his publishing job in the city. "Bonnemaman" stayed home, saw the children off to school, took care of the house, and was there when Tom and John Paul returned in the afternoon. Living in the Jenkinses' household gave Tom a new sense of stability.

Tom began to explore the neighborhood and made friends with several of the boys living nearby. Together they formed a "gang" and built a "headquarters" from boards and tar paper they had collected at construction sites. The gang was really more like a club, an innocent diversion created for fun, with no intentions of violence.

When Tom's friends weren't around, John Paul became Tom's co-conspirator in boyhood pranks: "There is no need to go into details of the trouble my brother and I often managed to create in the Douglaston household. When guests came whom we did not like [for example], we would hide under the tables, or run upstairs and throw hard and soft objects down into the hall and into the living room."

On days when there was no school, Tom liked to accompany his grandfather to Grosset & Dunlap, the book-publishing firm where he worked. There, Tom wandered through the huge showrooms filled with novels and children's books. He delighted in the fact that he "could go and curl up in a leather armchair and read all day without being disturbed." Reading had become one of Tom's favorite pastimes; history books, mysteries, and adventure stories fed Tom's eager imagination, expanded his vocabulary, and comforted him when he felt lonely and bored. In the journals he would keep later, Tom wrote about his favorite books as if they were people; he considered them among his finest teachers and most cherished friends.

Mealtime in the Jenkinses' household was always interesting. Pop had a boisterous nature and loved to talk. Bonnemaman was more reserved, but she shared her husband's enthusiasm for modern forms of entertainment, particularly the movies. Over dinner, they frequently discussed their favorite subject: the lives of the famous film stars Douglas Fairbanks and Mary Pickford. The Jenkinses, like many Americans at this time, were fascinated with Hollywood and its glamorous personalities. According to Tom, the acting team of Fairbanks and Pickford (who were, in real life, husband and wife) represented "every possible human ideal . . . beauty and wit, majesty, grace, and decorum, bravery and love, . . . truth, justice, honor, piety, loyalty, . . . and, above all, marital fidelity." The Jenkinses not only discussed the events of these two actors' lives but considered them "gods," Tom explained in *The Seven Storey Mountain*. "My grandfather's favorite place of worship was the Capitol theatre, in New York. When the [more modern] Roxy theatre was built, he transferred his allegiance [there] . . . and later on there was no shrine that so stirred his devotion as the Music Hall."

Tom's grandparents were vaguely Protestant, but they never went to church. "Bonnemaman used to read the little black books of Mary Baker Eddy [the founder of the Christian Science Church]," Tom wrote, "and I suppose that was the closest she got to religion." Pop's membership in the local chapter of the Masons (a secret fraternity whose purpose was to promote good works and charity) represented his version of spirituality.

It was from some of his Masonic friends, Tom supposed, that Pop developed his deep-seated prejudice against Catholics. After meetings, the men discussed politics and swapped stories about crooked New York politicians. Because several of these dishonest politicians were Catholic, Pop came to associate Catholics with corruption. It was a prejudice that Tom, who was too young to understand the danger of stereotypes, unconsciously assumed. "I did not know precisely what the word [Catholicism] meant," he recalled. "It only conveyed a kind of cold and unpleasant feeling."

While Tom and John Paul enjoyed the stable, contented life of middle-class American boys, their father was busy traveling and painting. Letters arrived in Douglaston from such distant places as southern France, Spain, and Algeria, on the northern coast of Africa. Then one day a letter arrived from one of Owen's friends, explaining that their father was gravely ill and "was, in fact, dying." Having lost their mother just three years before, the boys now faced the possibility of becoming orphaned. "I was profoundly affected, filled with sorrow and with fear," Tom wrote. "Was I never to see my father again?"

Owen Merton was delirious for days, and then — almost miraculously — began to recover. After he was back on his feet, he finished some more paintings. When he at last felt well enough to travel, he gathered his work and went to London. There he had another successful exhibition in the spring of 1925, his most successful one thus far. He sailed for New York immediately afterward, apparently healthy and anxious to see his sons.

But as Tom watched his father get off the ship in New York Harbor, he saw "a very different person . . . from the man who had taken me to Bermuda two years before." Owen Merton was much thinner now, and much of his face was covered by a thick, dark beard. Tom didn't like his father's new look at all. "When are you going to shave it off?" he inquired about the beard. "I'm not," replied his father.

Later that evening, Tom's father took him aside and announced his plans. "We are going to France," he told Tom, who almost immediately "burst into tears." Tom's feelings were, understandably, mixed. He was glad to be reunited with his father, and he understood his father's need to travel and work. Yet he was happily settled in Douglaston. "After the unusual experience of remaining some two years in one place," Tom recalled, "I was glad to be there, and liked my friends, and liked to go swimming in the bay. I had been given a small camera with which I took pictures, which my uncle . . . [had] developed for me at the Pennsylvania Drug Store. . . . I possessed a baseball bat with the word 'Spaulding' burnt on it in large letters. I thought maybe I would like to become a Boy Scout."

Tom secretly hoped that his father might drop the plan after a while. But Owen Merton remained firm in his decision. Although he sympathized with Tom's feelings of attachment to Douglaston, his illness had forced him to reconsider his family responsibilities. He too felt a need for more stability, but he wasn't comfortable in America, nor could he adjust to the middle-class, suburban lifestyle of his in-laws. He had been educated in Europe and had done some of his best work there; now that painful memories of the First World War were fading, he believed that his art would flourish if he returned. This time, however, he planned to take Tom with him and build a home. When it was ready, John Paul would join them, and the Merton family would once again live under the same roof.

And so, on August 25, 1925, Tom and his father boarded a passenger ship bound for France. In his autobiography, Tom — known to those at Gethsemani as "Father Louis" — wrote, "Although I did not know it, and it would not have interested me then, [the day we left] was the Feast of St. Louis of France."

CHAPTER 4

European Roots

When he failed to change his father's mind, Tom tried to view his return to Europe more positively. He began to see it as yet another adventure — in the long succession of adventures — that he and his father would share.

Upon reaching France, the Mertons took a train from Paris to the southwest region of Languedoc. As they traveled, Tom felt a mixture of patriotism and pride as he noted the details of France's terrain, its people, and its architecture. "When I went to France, in 1925, returning to the land of my birth, I was also returning to the fountains of the intellectual and spiritual life of the world to which I belonged," he wrote in *The Seven Storey Mountain*.

The train took them through the mountainous regions of central France to the town of Montauban. After settling into a room at the local hotel, they felt restless and decided to take an evening walk. As they strolled along the narrow streets in the dim evening light, Tom had a strange feeling that he had been there before: "What a dead town!" he wrote. "And yet, instead of being dreary, it was pleasant. And although I had no conscious memory of anything like this, it was familiar, and I felt at home." Owen Merton also seemed happy to be back in France. He smiled more, and he kept taking deep breaths of the air, which smelled of woodsmoke and pine needles.

Tom also noticed that his father's attitude was different — both toward his children and toward his faith. "Whether it was his sickness or not, I do not know," Tom recalled, "but something had made him certain that he could not leave the training and care of his sons to other people. . . . And, what is more, he had become definitely aware of certain religious obligations for us as well as for himself. He told me to pray, to ask God to help us, to help him paint, to help him have a successful exhibition, to find us a place to live."

Tom's father had chosen Montauban as the city they should live in because several of his friends had recommended the Institute Jean Calvin, a nearby school that offered religious training for boys. But when Tom and his father visited the institute the following week, Owen Merton didn't like it, though he never told Tom exactly why.

They decided to move on in search of another town in which to settle. At the "Syndicat d'Initiative" (the tourist information center) in Montauban, Owen Merton had seen pictures of a town to the northeast — St. Antonin — and was attracted by its old buildings and tranquil streets. When he and Tom arrived there, they discovered that it was a thoroughly medieval town, complete with narrow, winding streets, stone fountains, and religious ruins. "To walk through those streets was to be in the Middle Ages," Tom wrote. "Nothing had been touched by man, only by ruin and by the passage of time." The one exception was the Catholic church, which stood in the center of the town and seemed to be the focal point not only of the town but of the surrounding area. "The whole landscape, unified by the church and its heavenward spire, seemed to say: 'this is the meaning of all created things: we have been made for no other purpose than that men may use us in proclaiming the glory of God.'"

Tom and his father decided to stay. Owen Merton rented a small apartment near the edge of town and began searching for a suitable place to build his own home. Tom accompanied him on these daylong expeditions, during which they explored ancient ruins, abandoned farmhouses, and woodland pathways. "We travelled all over the countryside looking at places, and also visiting villages where there might be good subjects for pictures," Tom wrote. "I was constantly in and out of old churches, and stumbled upon the ruins of ancient chapels and monasteries."

As they explored the countryside together, Owen Merton pointed out different features of land and water, and the various qualities of light that affected his choice of subjects and painting methods. He also shared his views on human spirituality and, more specifically, the merits of Catholicism. "I learned later from some of his friends," Tom recalled, "that at that time there had been not a little likelihood that he might become a Catholic. He seems to have been much attracted to the Church, but in the end he resisted the attraction because of the rest of us. . . . For . . . there might have been immense complications with the rest of the family."

Given this attraction, perhaps it was no accident that Owen Merton purchased some land near St. Antonin, which lay at the bottom of a hill known as "Le Calvaire" (Calvary). It had been named for the small, abandoned chapel that stood on top, the endpoint of "a series of shrines, making the Fourteen Stations of the Cross [the stages of Christ's passion and death] between the town and the top of the hill." This was to be the backdrop of Tom's new home, the plans for which his father was only too eager to begin.

In the fall, Tom attended the local elementary school, where he "sat with great embarassment among the very smallest children, and tried to [learn] French." His father, meanwhile, returned to his painting, supervised the construction of their house, laid out a large garden, and had a well dug. Next to the well he planted two poplar trees, one for Tom and another for John Paul.

The citizens of St. Antonin welcomed the young artist and his son into their community. Tom gradually

31

adjusted to school, and his French improved. When his American grandfather sent him some money for Christmas, he bought a set of books called *Le Pays de France (The Country of France)* and spent many hours reading about "all the other wonderful places there were" in his homeland. The pictures of religious buildings — cathedrals, churches, monasteries, and cloisters — claimed his interest in a way that nothing before ever had. He was particularly taken by the picture of the "huddled buildings of the ancient Grande Chartreuse, crowded together in their solitary valley," he remembered. "What kind of men had lived in those cells? [At that time] I had no curiosity about monastic vocations or religious rules, but I know my heart was filled with a kind of longing to breathe the air of that lonely valley and to listen to its silence. I wanted to be in all these places. . . . Indeed, it was a kind of problem to me and an unconscious source of obscure and half-realized woe, that I could not be in all of them at once." Tom's interest in quiet, solitary places would surface frequently in the next decade, and eventually draw him to consider a life similar to that of the men in his picturebooks.

Tom's respect for his father grew with each passing week as he began to understand the sacrifices his father made in order to pursue his career. Owen Merton worked long hours in relative obscurity, isolated from his colleagues, and had little financial compensation. His profession required a certain amount of faith and vision, as well as tremendous dedication. Like all successful painters, Tom's father honored the artistic traditions of those who had preceded him, while remaining loyal to his own definitions of beauty and truth. Years later, Tom would emulate his father by attempting to structure his writing life in a similar manner. Only then would he realize how deeply his father had influenced him, and how much their adult lives had in common.

In the summer of 1926, Pop had decided that he, Bonnemaman, and John Paul would come for a visit. So he had "gathered up a great mountain of baggage" in New York and, with his wife and Tom's brother in tow, "boarded the liner *Leviathan* and started for Europe." But he had no interest in staying in St. Antonin. "He wanted to keep on the move," Tom wrote, "and since he had two months at his disposal, he saw no reason why he could not cover the whole of Europe." Although he eventually scaled back this grand ambition, he was determined to see England, Switzerland, and France.

After a frenzied tour of England, Pop, Bonnemaman, and John Paul met Tom and his father in Paris. Since Pop's next goal was to "see" Switzerland, his four fellow travelers found themselves reluctant passengers on train rides lasting seven or eight hours, punctuated by short stays in several Swiss towns. Things went from bad to worse. On the day they went up the Jungfrau mountain by train, Tom recalled, "everybody was ready to fall down from nervous exhaustion, and the height made Bonnemaman faint, and Pop began to feel sick, and I had a big crisis of tears." At the hotel in Interlaken, "John Paul humiliated the whole family by falling fully dressed into a pond full of gold-fish and running through the hotel dripping with water and green-weeds." Everyone was glad to return to France, even the adventurous Tom, who at this point was bored and fatigued: "By the time we reached Avignon, I had developed such a disgust for sightseeing that I would not leave the hotel . . . [but] remained in the room and read *Tarzan of the Apes*."

Pop, Bonnemaman, and John Paul returned to the United States at the end of August. For Tom, their visit had been marred by all the "miserable" traveling, but he was grateful that he had been able to see them once again.

In September, Tom began school at the lycée (French secondary school) in Montauban, the one closest to St. Antonin. At this all-boys boarding school, students slept in dormitories during the week and were allowed to return home on weekends. The atmosphere of the lycée, however, was far less friendly than that of the elementary school in St. Antonin. Eleven-year-old Tom was one of the newcomers, and — not being a native of the region — was considered an "outsider." Right from the start, he found himself the object of teasing, bullying, and malicious pranks by the older students. "They kick[ed] me, and [began] to pull and twist my ears, and push me around, and shout various kinds of insults," Tom wrote in *The Seven Storey Mountain*. "I learned a great deal of obscenity and blasphemy in the first few days, simply by being the direct or indirect object of so much of it."

The situation improved after the other boys got used to "my pale, blue-eyed and seemingly stupid English face," Tom noted, but he remained lonely and homesick: "When I lay awake at night in the huge dark dormitory and listened to the snoring of the little animals [the bullying boys] all around me, and heard through the darkness and the emptiness of the night the far screaming of the trains, . . . I knew for the first time in my life the pangs of desolation and emptiness and abandonment."

For the first several weeks Tom went home almost every weekend and begged his father to "let [him] out of that miserable school." But it was no use. Owen was restricted by finances and geography; if Tom was going to receive an education, there was little choice about where he could go. "After about two months," Tom recalled, "I got used to it and ceased to be so unhappy. The wound was no longer so raw: but I was never happy or at peace in the violent and unpleasant atmosphere of those brick cloisters."

What made matters worse was "the tyranny of Monsieur le Proviseur and his henchman, Monsieur le Censeur," according to Michael Mott, author of *The Seven Mountains of Thomas Merton*. "In the pull between order and freedom, the school in Montauban provided the worst of both — a combination of regimentation and chaos." Years later, when Tom wrote a novel called *My Argument with the Gestapo,* he used the school administrators as models for the two most despicable characters in the story.

But one thing eventually got better: Tom found a few friends his own age with whom he enjoyed spending time. Like Tom, these boys were adventurous, creative, and intellectually curious. "I remember we were all furiously writing novels," Tom recalled. "On the days when we [he and his classmates] went out for walks, two by two into the country . . ., my friends and I would get together, walking in a superior way, with our caps on the backs of our heads and our hands in our pockets, like the great intellectuals that we were, discussing our novels." They not only talked about plots but also offered criticisms of each other's work.

These early literary experiments were significant in Tom's development as a creative thinker and, later, in his vocation as a writer. Like his father, who frequently sought the support and companionship of other artists, Tom learned to seek the advice and friendship of other writers.

As the weather turned colder and the dampness settled into the stone walls of the lycée, Tom's health began to suffer. He took fewer long walks into the countryside and spent more nights in the infirmary, trying to sleep between bouts of coughing. The "wolf-pack" (the nickname Tom had given to the older boys) showed no sympathy for his illness, and continued to intimidate him.

Tom's rescue came in December. His father had gone to do some painting in the farmlands of the Central Mountains over the Christmas holidays. Tom could join him there for a few weeks if he wanted to.

Tom agreed, unaware that he would soon meet two people who would greatly influence his life.

CHAPTER 5

Escape to England

The first weeks of December passed all too slowly. When the holiday finally arrived, Tom took the first train to Murat, a small town nestled in the picturesque "Massif Central" (central mountains) in the province of Auvergne. His picturebooks had described Auvergne as one of the oldest settled regions of France, and its people as devoted Catholics who respected religious traditions. "The town [of Murat] huddled at the foot of a rock crowned by a colossal statue of the Immaculate Conception," Tom remembered. "These people wanted to say in a very obvious way that they loved [the Virgin Mary] . . . as a Queen of great power and a Lady of immense goodness and mercy."

Tom's father met him at the train station and took him to the farmhouse where he was staying. The farm was owned by the Privats, an elderly couple who led a simple, hardworking life. "In a way, they were to be among the most remarkable people I ever knew," Tom wrote in *The Seven Storey Mountain*. "I remember their kindness and goodness to me, and their peacefulness and their utter simplicity. They inspired real reverence, and I think, in a way, they were certainly saints. And they were saints in that most effective and telling way: sanctified by leading ordinary lives in a completely supernatural manner. . . . Their farm, their family, and their Church were all that occupied these good souls; and their lives were full."

The Privats' warmth and friendliness provided a welcome change from the cold and repressive atmosphere of the lycée. Each day, while his father painted the quaint mountain scenes, Tom helped Monsieur Privat tend to the animals — horses, cows, goats, and chickens — and assisted him with various chores and repairs. As they worked, Tom studied the old man, searching for clues to his peaceful, contented nature, his sense of inner strength. "He was tremendously broad, a man of great [physical] strength," Tom recalled. "He seemed to have no neck, but his head rose from his shoulders in a solid column of muscle and bone. . . . He wore a black broad-brimmed hat, like most of the peasants of the region, and . . . his sober and judicious eyes looked out at you peacefully from under the regular brows and that regular brim above them. These . . . two levels of regularity added much to the impression of solidity . . . and impassiveness which he carried with him everywhere, whether at work or at rest."

Madame Privat was a small, thin woman whose traditional Auvergnat headdress looked "like a little sugar-loaf perched on top of her head." Tom had a hearty appetite for her cooking, and a deep appreciation for the kindness she showered upon him. Like her husband, she possessed great inner strength and, as Tom later explained, was "full of that peacefulness and impassiveness which, as I now know, came from living close to God."

Tom returned to the lycée after the holidays. His health had improved, so he was allowed to go home on weekends. In St. Antonin, he watched the carpenters and masons put the finishing touches on the new house. "It was a beautiful little house," he recalled, "simple and solid. It looked good to live in, with that one big room with the medieval window and a huge medieval fireplace. Father had even managed to procure a winding stone stair[case]."

Unfortunately, Owen Merton's work frequently took him away from St. Antonin. At the urging of his colleagues, who feared that he was becoming too isolated in St. Antonin, he spent the summer of 1927 traveling along the southern coast of France, painting Mediterranean landscapes. Once again, Tom's father felt torn between his duty to his family and his commitment to art. He longed to give Tom and John Paul a permanent home and to establish a sense of family unity that had eluded them since his wife's death. Yet he was deeply committed to his work and knew he must listen to those who had influence at the galleries and exhibitions where his paintings were sold.

Fortunately, Owen Merton had arranged for Tom to stay with the Privats while he was away. Tom never forgot this second visit. He ran in the woods and climbed the mountains nearby, and he talked about school and his travels with his father. He remembered discussing religion with the Privats only once — but he remembered the conversation vividly. As they were watching the sun set one night, Tom declared, "Every man should go according to his own conscience, and settle things according to his own private way of looking at things." The Privats were stunned. "Mais c'est impossible," Monsieur Privat responded, speaking for him and his wife. They didn't believe that individuals could find God outside of formal Christianity — specifically, Catholicism. They were "concerned, . . . so deeply and vitally concerned, at my lack of faith," Tom wrote. But they did not punish him or lecture him about his beliefs. Instead, they prayed that Tom would someday realize his need to commit himself, as they had committed themselves, to a Christian life. "Who knows how much I owe to these two wonderful people?" Tom wrote many years later, after joining the Trappists. "I owe many graces to their prayers, and perhaps ultimately the grace of my conversion and even of my religious vocation."

That fall, Tom returned to the lycée, and his father continued to travel. During his second year at the school, Tom recalled, he was "becoming more and more hard-boiled in my precocity, and getting accustomed to the idea of growing up as a Frenchman." But then, after a successful exhibition in London in the spring of 1928, Owen Merton made a surprise visit to the school and told Tom to pack his bags — they were going to England.

Tom couldn't believe his ears. "I looked around me like a man that has had chains struck from his hands. How the light sang on the brick walls of the prison whose gates had just burst open before me." Although Tom was happy to be leaving the lycée, he was a bit sad that he and his father never actually lived in the house in St. Antonin. Still, he was with his father again. And Owen Merton was now striking a compromise between work and family that he hoped would lessen the conflict between his passion for painting and his devotion to his children.

Father and son traveled by train through France, then took a steamboat across the English Channel, arriving in Dover on England's southern coast. Tom's first impression of Great Britain was "the smell of strong tea in the station refreshment room" and the "cockney cries of the porters" who unloaded their bags. Tom and his father took a second train to London, then a third to the quiet suburb of Ealing, where Owen's Aunt Maud and Uncle Benjamin Pearce lived in a neat red-brick house.

Tom was intimidated by his great-uncle Benjamin, a "stoop-shouldered man with a huge, white waterfall mustache" who had recently retired as headmaster of a local boys' school. But his Aunt Maud was a sweet-tempered woman whose comforting presence made Tom feel safe, welcome, and respected. "I have met very few people in my life so like an angel," Tom wrote.

It was with Aunt Maud that Tom had his first serious discussion about careers. When they were riding home on the bus from a shopping excursion to London, Aunt Maud pondered out loud, "I wonder if Tom has thought at all about his future." Tom knew that most adults would expect a practical answer, so he was reluctant to share his recent thoughts about becoming a novelist. Instead, he asked her what she thought about a career in writing. Aunt Maud gave a very tactful answer: she considered writing "a very fine profession," she said, but she gently reminded Tom that writers often found it difficult to make a living. Without discouraging him from writing altogether, she helped him form a plan that would develop his practical skills but not destroy his dreams. "I might be a journalist and write for newspapers," Tom suggested while they were discussing various writing careers. "And I could write books in my spare time." Aunt Maud nodded her approval. "A knowledge of languages would be very valuable in that field," she added.

A few weeks later, Tom was enrolled at Ripley Court, a boys' boarding school in Surrey where Uncle Ben's sister-in-law was headmistress. "She was a bulky and rather belligerent-looking woman, with great pouches under her eyes," Tom remembered. On the day he met with her at the school, his Aunt Maud was with him.

When Aunt Maud told Mrs. Pearce that Tom was think-ing of becoming a journalist, she replied, "There's no use in his wasting his time and deceiving himself. He might as well get some sensible ideas into his head from the very start, and prepare himself for something solid and reliable and not go out into the world with his head full of dreams." Fortunately, Mrs. Pearce had little in-fluence over Tom's schooling, and he ignored her bad advice.

Tom entered Ripley in the early fall of 1928 and was immediately happy there. Unlike the "wolf-pack" at Montauban, the Ripley students were generally cheer-ful, friendly, and tolerant of newcomers. Most of the boys were from comfortable, middle-class homes, which shielded them from "the harsh realities of the world in the late 1920s." Tom's unconventional child-hood — the fact that he had lived in America, Bermuda, and France — and the fact that his father was an artist (and not a doctor, lawyer, or businessman) set him apart from his fellow students. But the Ripley boys, instead of mocking him, included him in their circle of friends; they were impressed by his worldliness.

At Ripley, Tom learned to play soccer (which he liked) and cricket (which he disliked), and he began the difficult task of learning Latin. The French schools had not required the study of classical languages, so Tom was a few years behind. In other subjects, however, he performed exceptionally well and needed little en-couragement to study. He continued to read novels and adventure stories on his own, developing a preference for Sherlock Holmes mysteries by Sir Arthur Conan Doyle and novels such as *Oliver Twist* and *A Christmas Carol* by Charles Dickens.

On Sundays Tom attended the local Anglican church. Kneeling down beside his classmates in the long, wooden pews, he "began to pray with real feeling" for the first time. There were opportunities for daily worship, too. At school the students said a prayer before each meal, and again just before bedtime. Many considered prayer simply another drill to be endured. Tom, however, was deeply affected: "Just about the time when I most needed it, I did acquire a little natural faith," he wrote in his autobiography, "and found many occasions of praying and lifting up my mind to God. . . . And for about the next two years I think I was almost sincerely religious."

The year at Ripley was passing quickly. At fourteen, Tom was now old enough for public school. (In England, "public" schools are private, college-prep academies.) Despite his excellent academic record, Tom's "late start" in Latin (and his father's financial status) stood in the way of his getting a scholarship to Eton or Harrow, two of the best prep schools in England. Instead, Aunt Maud and Uncle Ben recommended Oakham, a smaller, less competitive academy in the English Midlands.

Tom's father agreed with their choice but wondered how he would pay the tuition. He then received a letter from his father-in-law, who offered to pay Tom's expenses. Owen Merton accepted gratefully, unaware that Pop's financial generosity would soon take on an even greater importance.

For just as Tom's life began to stabilize, just as he was becoming comfortable with his new friends and the rituals and routines of English boarding school, tragedy struck once again. On a warm June day near the end of the summer term at Ripley, when Tom accompanied the school's cricket team to a game in Ealing, he was told that his father was at his Aunt Maud's house, and was ill. Since no one summoned him with any real urgency, Tom assumed that nothing was seriously wrong with his father. But when he made his way to the house at tea time, he saw otherwise. "Father was in bed. You could not tell from his appearance how ill he was: but I managed to gather it from the way he talked and from his actions," Tom remembered. "He seemed to move with difficulty and pain, and he did not have much to say. When I asked him what was the matter, he said nobody seemed to know."

Tom returned to school worried and depressed about his father's condition. Aunt Maud wrote reassuring letters, saying that his father had placed himself in the hands of Tom Bennett, his longtime friend and a respected doctor at London's Middlesex Hospital. Bennett was also Tom's godfather, a fact that would become more important as Owen's illness progressed.

Following Bennett's advice, Owen Merton stopped painting and rested as much as possible. At the end of the school term, he took Tom to Scotland, where he had accepted an invitation to stay at the home of some friends, the Haughtons, near Aberdeen. There he hoped to regain his strength, enjoy the summer holiday with his son, and return to England refreshed.

Within the first week, however, Tom realized that his father was getting worse: "For the first few days Father kept to his room, coming down for meals. Once or twice he went out into the garden. Soon he could not even come down for meals." The local doctor was called in, but his medicines proved ineffective. He advised Owen to go to the hospital in London, where a diagnosis could be made and more effective treatment provided.

Tom recalled the day his father announced that he was going to return to London. "Pray God to make me well," he asked Tom. Then he suggested that Tom stay with the Haughtons for the rest of the summer. "They are very nice. They will take good care of you, and it will do you good."

Owen Merton had said he thought he would be all right "in due course," but Tom was deeply worried. The "sincerely religious" feelings he had begun to have seemed to vanish in the face of his father's illness. How could God — who was supposed to be all-knowing and all-loving — allow this to happen? Tom wondered. He felt helpless, alone, and afraid. Reluctantly, he saw his father off on the train, then returned with the Haughtons, hoping to make friends with their two teenage daughters.

But he quickly discovered that the Haughton girls

were more interested in their horses than they were in him. Tom was eager for company, so he tried to appear interested in horses, too. He soon became bored, however, and spent most of each day reading novels by the French author Alexandre Dumas that he borrowed from the Haughtons' library.

One afternoon, when he was alone in the house and absorbed in his reading, the telephone rang. Tom answered it, expecting to take a message for one of the Haughtons. Instead, a Scottish woman at the local telegraph office read a message addressed to him: "Entering New York Harbor. All well," it said. "At first I could not make out [her] words," Tom recalled. "Then, when I did make them out, I did not believe them. . . . [The message] came from Father, in the hospital, in London. I tried to argue . . . that it came from my Uncle Harold, who had been traveling in Europe that year. But [the woman] would not be argued into anything but what she saw right in front of her nose."

Dazed, Tom hung up and shuffled slowly around the empty house. He knew the message could mean only one thing: his father was losing his mind. "The bottom dropped out of my stomach," Tom wrote. "I sat down in one of the big leather chairs in the smoking room. . . . I sat there in the dark, unhappy room, unable to think, unable to move, with all the . . . elements of my isolation crowding in upon me from every side: without a home, without a family, without a country, [and now] without a father."

When Tom returned to Ealing, his Uncle Ben gave him the dire news the minute he walked into the house: Tom's father had a malignant brain tumor. Tom went to the hospital at once. He found his father lucid (he didn't mention the telegram), though still terribly weak. "He told me that they were going to try and operate on him," Tom recalled, "but they were afraid they could not do very much. Again he told me to pray."

Tom set off for Oakham in September of 1929. (It is very likely that his Aunt Maud and Uncle Ben thought his life should go on as usual even though his father was sick.) The excitement of a new environment and the demands of the school routine temporarily distracted him from his father's illness. He felt at home among Oakham's old stone buildings and made new friends easily. John Barber, who later became a teacher and headmaster at Oakham, was one of Tom's first acquaintances. "The culture of the average lad [there] wasn't all that deep," Barber told Paul Wilkes, who produced a film on Merton's life. "Many of them came here for, say, three years, and left . . . to go into business or work with their fathers on the farm, but that was about it." Although Tom's background made him quite different, Barber commented that "as far as friendship was concerned, that was all on the level. We got on very well with him because he was such a great chap." In *The Seven Storey Mountain*, Tom recalled how he and his friends used to amuse themselves: "Pop used to send me the brown rotogravure sections of the New York

Sunday papers, and we would cut out the pictures of the actresses and paste them up on the walls. . . . And we drank raisin wine and ate potato chips until we fell silent and sat apart, stupefied and nauseated."

The first-year students endured some taunting and bullying by the upperclassmen, but after the horrors of Montauban, Tom considered this a comparatively harmless school-boy tradition. His classes now included nineteenth-century European history, English literature, Greek, Latin, religion, and trigonometry. His voracious appetite for reading helped him to excel in literature and history; Greek and Latin also came more easily, now that he had mastered the basics. But math was a struggle. "Buggy Jerwood, the school chaplain, tried to teach us trigonometry," Tom wrote. "[But] with me, he failed." Tom's verbal proficiency clearly surpassed his numerical skills; despite his best efforts, he would continue to struggle in math courses for the remainder of his school days.

Religious teaching at Oakham was different from anything else Tom had experienced. Classes were taught by Buggy Jerwood, whose instruction consisted mostly of "more or less vague ethical remarks, an obscure mixture of ideals of English gentlemanliness and his favorite notions of personal hygiene." During one of his lessons, the chaplain suggested substituting "all that we mean when we call a chap a 'gentleman'" for the word "charity" wherever it appeared in St. Paul's letter in 1 Corinthians 13. "In other words," Tom wrote, "charity [in the Bible] meant good-sportsman-ship, cricket, the decent thing, wearing the right kind of clothes, using the proper spoon, not being a cad or a bounder."

Outside of class, Tom took up boxing, participated in army training maneuvers (always with a book in his pocket), and wrote letters to his brother in New York and to his father in London.

During this first busy year, Tom seldom saw his father. But he would see him in June, and then he would confront the fear that underlay all his schoolboy's activity — the fear that his father would not recover.

CHAPTER 6

A Searching Time

In June of 1930, Tom's brother and grandparents came from the United States for a visit. The Great Depression of the 1920s had changed Pop's perspective on spending, and the Jenkins family "no longer took towns by storm." Instead, they stayed at the modestly priced Crown Inn near Oakham.

Shortly after they arrived, Pop took Tom aside to discuss the family finances. Publishing had survived the decade better than many businesses, Sam Jenkins explained, and he was "not altogether ruined." He had lost some of his investments, but he had retained ownership of a few parcels of real estate, some shares of stock in American manufacturing companies, and the life-insurance policies he had purchased for Tom and John Paul.

Tom listened carefully. Because his father could no longer take care of him, he would have to learn how to plan for and manage his own future. "I understood that I ought to be able to get along all right until about 1940," he recalled. "When it was all done, Pop gave me the piece of paper with all the figures on it . . . and said: 'So now it's all settled. No matter what happens to me, you will . . . be taken care of.'" This exchange made a lasting impression on Tom: "I think it was the first time in my life I had ever been treated as if I were completely grown up and able to take care of myself."

Pop then further surprised the fifteen-year-old. Although Pop had always detested smoking, he announced that he was in favor of Tom's smoking (something Tom had been doing secretively for a while), and he actually bought Tom a pipe. When Tom realized that this was his grandfather's way of recognizing his maturity, he accepted it gratefully.

In addition to giving Tom his financial independence, Pop changed Tom's "home base" in England. Up until this point, Tom had spent his school holidays and vacations with his Aunt Maud and Uncle Ben in Ealing, or with Gwyneth Trier — his father's younger sister — in West Horsley. But from now on, Tom would stay with his godfather, Tom Bennett, at his apartment on Harvey Street in the center of London. There were two reasons for this: Tom would be exposed to cultural opportunities — chances to experience art, music, and theater — that the suburbs didn't provide; and it would be easier for Tom to visit his father in Middlesex Hospital, which was located in London.

Of course, one of the principal reasons that Pop had

brought Bonnemaman and John Paul to London was so that they could see Owen Merton in the hospital. That summer, in fact, Tom stayed with them in London, and together they visited his father often. Tom's memories of the first visit were poignantly vivid. "When I saw him, I knew at once there was no hope of his living much longer," he wrote. "His face was swollen. His eyes were not clear but, above all, the tumor had raised a tremendous swelling on his forehead." Even though Owen Merton could no longer speak, he could comprehend what Tom was saying to him. Still, Tom recalled, "the sorrow of his great helplessness suddenly fell upon me like a mountain. I was crushed by it. The tears sprang to my eyes. . . . I hid my face in the blanket and cried. And poor Father wept, too. The others stood by. It was excruciatingly sad. We were completely helpless. There was nothing anyone could do."

Although coping with the imminent loss of his father must have been very difficult for Tom, he returned to Oakham in the fall and "plunged into everything with equal energy," according to biographer Michael Mott. The new headmaster, F. C. Doherty, recognized Tom's exceptional academic ability right away. He convinced Tom to begin preparing for the Higher Certificate (the more difficult of the two diplomas offered in public schools), which would make him eligible for a scholarship at the most competitive universities. The Higher Certificate was hard to obtain, Doherty explained, but if Tom specialized in foreign languages, he would not be required to study advanced mathematics. This, of course, suited Tom just fine.

Under Doherty's guidance, Tom progressed rapidly and was in the equivalent of the sixth form (roughly the eleventh grade) by the middle of his second year. Tom's swift intellectual ascent was tragically paralleled by his father's physical decline. The doctors could do nothing more, and each visit to the hospital left Tom more and more depressed. There was one consolation, however. During the long months when his father lay helplessly in the hospital, struggling courageously against the cancer, he turned his mind more frequently to God. One day when Tom came to visit, he found his father's bed covered with "little sheets of blue note-paper" on which he had drawn "saints with beards and great halos" — drawings "unlike anything he had ever done before," Tom recalled. He believed that God gave his father "light to understand and to make use of his suffering for his own good, and to perfect his soul . . . [so that] this terrible and frightening illness . . . was not destroying him after all."

At this point, however, this realization did little to ease Tom's pain. "What could I make of so much suffering?" he wrote. "There was no way for me . . . to get anything out of it. It was a raw wound for which there was no adequate relief."

During the Christmas holidays, Tom spent most of his time in Germany, where his godfather had arranged for him to stay with a family friend, but he did see his father once or twice. He had been back at Oakham for just a week when the headmaster called him into his office and gave him a telegram. It said that Owen Merton had just died in Middlesex Hospital; the date was January 18, 1931. "The sorry business was all over. And my mind made nothing of it," Tom wrote. "There was nothing I seemed to be able to grasp. Here was a man with a wonderful mind and a great talent and a great heart; and, what was more, he was the man who had brought me into the world, and had nourished me and cared for me and had shaped my soul and to whom I was bound by every possible kind of bond of affection and attachment and admiration and reverence: killed by a growth on his brain."

Tom's godfather made the funeral arrangements, wrote an obituary for the London *Times,* and attended the church service and cremation with Tom.

Back at school, Tom fought his grief by throwing himself zealously into his studies. He had begun to read the poetry of William Blake (1757-1827), the English artist and philosopher whose "strongly religious nature came to identify Art . . . with Christianity." Blake had been a favorite of Owen Merton, who had "tried to explain [to Tom] what was good about him" when they were living in St. Antonin. At that time, Tom hadn't understood his father's explanation. But now, at age sixteen, he found himself "astounded" and "moved" by the Englishman's mystical poetry.

Several years later, Blake's work would become the

subject of Tom's master's thesis at Columbia University. By the time Tom wrote *The Seven Storey Mountain,* he realized that he still hadn't had the capacity to truly understand Blake when he was a young student. "How incapable I was of understanding anything like the ideals of a William Blake! How could I possibly realize that his rebellion . . . was fundamentally the rebellion of the saints. It was the rebellion of the lover of the living God. . . . His faith was so real and his love for God so mighty and so sincere." This pure love of God, which Blake seemed to have, was a virtue that Tom would struggle to attain throughout his life in the monastery.

Over the next several months, Tom's sadness over his father's death ebbed away. "And when it did," he wrote, "I found myself completely stripped of everything that impeded the movement of my own will to do as it pleased. I imagined that I was free." It was this false sense of freedom and interest in satisfying his appetites that began to shape Tom's life.

During the Easter holiday, Tom decided to spend the time alone — and to travel by himself. He went to Rome and Florence, probably expecting to be dazzled — but instead he was disappointed. He traveled by himself again that summer, taking an ocean liner to New York to visit his brother and grandparents. He bought the ticket himself and wore "a brand-new suit" for the occasion. Once again Tom had great hopes: "On the boat

I am going to meet a beautiful girl, and I am going to fall in love," he said to himself. These were high expectations for a ten-day trip, but Tom was young, innocent, and full of romantic notions that had not been tested in the real world.

On the fourth day, he glimpsed a lovely female passenger strolling along the deck and immediately developed a crush on her. Then the Catholic priest "who knew everybody on the boat" introduced her to Tom. Her name was Norma Wakefield. To Tom's "dazzled eyes," she became "the heroine of every novel." "I all but flung myself face down on the deck at her feet," he remembered. "She could have put a collar on my neck and led me around from that time forth on the end of a chain." Before they reached New York, Tom declared his "undying love." There was, it seems, just a single kiss before Norma — who was nearly twice Tom's age — told him gently but firmly that he was too young for her, and that she would not be seeing him again.

Devastated by her rejection, Tom returned to his cabin and "sobbed over [his] diary." It was a painful but necessary lesson: from now on, his exaggerated notions of romance would be replaced by more realistic expectations.

When his family met him at the dock, Tom felt awful: "With my heart ready to explode with immature emotions I suddenly found myself surrounded by all the cheerful and peaceful and comfortable solicitudes of home." His grandparents tried to cheer him up by giving him a tour of New York, but it didn't work. After that they allowed him to work out his feelings of grief, abandonment, and adolescent frustration in his own way. Tom remained moody and somewhat withdrawn for the rest of the summer.

He sailed back to England in September, spending the week before school began at the Bennetts' stylish London apartment. According to biographer Monica Furlong, author of *Merton: A Biography*, both Tom Bennett and his wife, Iris, "a petite and elegant Frenchwoman, lived with style and sophistication and with a knowledge of all that was most new and exciting in European culture." The Bennetts' apartment was decorated with original oil paintings and expensive antiques. A maid served Tom breakfast in bed and did his laundry and ironing. Lunch and dinner were served in the elegant dining room, on a "little table" that made Tom "afraid to move for fear the whole thing would collapse and the pretty French dishes would smash on the floor." After the quaint countryside charm of Oakham and the simple suburban lifestyle of Douglaston, the Bennetts' London flat seemed part of another world.

In the absence of parents or grandparents, Tom's godfather — who was now his guardian as well — became his next logical role model. The doctor had a far more sophisticated lifestyle than Tom was used to, but Tom tried hard to understand it and to become a part of his godfather's world. When he visited during holidays, Tom studied his godfather's preferences for certain foods, styles of clothing, and forms of entertainment; then he tried to copy them. He read novels by authors that Bennett recommended — Ernest Hemingway, James Joyce, D. H. Lawrence, and André Gide — and bought recordings of music that Bennett liked. (At one point his godfather told Tom that Maurice Ravel's *Bolero* was "phony.") Even Tom's tastes in art and film were affected: his godfather took him to exhibits that featured the paintings of Marc Chagall and "several others like him," and introduced him to Russian movies.

During this period, Tom was experiencing his life on two levels. On one level, he was broadening his cultural knowledge under Tom and Iris Bennett's influence and developing his intellectual skills at Oakham. On another level, however, he still wrestled with feelings of emptiness over his father's death, suffered keenly from teenage awkwardness (he was tall for his age, and he found girls attractive but intimidating), and was generally confused about who he was, what he believed in, and where he was headed. Often he imagined himself as the main character in one of the novels he was reading, as someone living a life of complete freedom and daring, repeatedly falling in love, yet uncommitted to a single person, belief system, or humanitarian cause. In moderation, these fantasies are a normal part of growing up. But having few authentic role models to emulate, Tom took them more seriously and more literally than he should have. "I became the complete twentieth-century man," Tom recalled in his autobiography. "I now belonged to the world in which I lived."

Despite his emotional self-doubts and shaky sense of personal identity, Tom's academic performance remained excellent. He won English prizes and became editor of the school magazine, *The Oakhamian*. In addition to overseeing its production, he regularly contributed drawings, articles, essays, and poems. Many of these centered on controversial social issues such as India's struggle for independence (England ruled India until 1947), Hitler's rise to power in Europe, and the co-existence of extreme poverty and great wealth in European and American cities.

He participated in school debates, often adopting the less popular position. In a debate regarding England's adoption of a national government, for example, "T. F. Merton," according to Oakham's records, "adopted the Socialist point of view, mentioning the panacea of nationalism"; his side lost, 38 votes to 6.

But Tom seemed comfortable playing the role of the underdog. He didn't mind facing criticism, and he enjoyed the challenge of presenting a new perspective on old problems. This tendency toward individualism and creative thinking could probably be credited in part to the example that his parents had set for him. As young artists, they had pursued their own goals and dreams, no matter what other people thought. Tom's ability to face adversity, to hold fast to his opinions despite sharp opposition, grew stronger as he grew older. When he became a writer, he used it frequently to uphold his right to express controversial opinions while remaining loyal to the Catholic Church.

Tom attained the Higher Certificate in September of 1932. He then took the scholarship exam for Cambridge University and was admitted to its Clare College division in December. Classes didn't begin until the following fall, so Tom was eager to test the boundaries of his personal freedom. "Now, at last, I imagined that I really was grown up and independent, and I could stretch out my hands and take all the things I wanted," he wrote. But true freedom, Tom would soon discover, required a certain degree of maturity that he didn't yet possess.

First he went overboard in his attempt to savor all the delights of the Christmas holidays: "I ate and drank so much and went to so many parties that I made myself sick," he remembered. Then, at the end of January, he embarked on an extended vacation to Italy — only to realize that his money would run out before he even got to Genoa. He had to write his godfather for more funds so that he could continue his travels.

Like his first romantic encounter, which had ended in humiliation and disillusionment, Tom's first taste of adult independence was not quite what he had imagined it would be. Even his godfather, whose lifestyle was fairly self-indulgent, scolded Tom in responding to his request for money: Mr. Bennett chided him for his lack of discipline and his failure to live within reasonable financial limits. "So after a month of my precious liberty, I received my first indication that my desires could never be absolute," Tom wrote. "They must necessarily be conditioned and modified by contacts and conflicts with the desires and interests of others. This was something that it would take me a long time to find out."

Despite his godfather's rebuke, Tom spent the entire spring traveling through Europe, taking long train rides, visiting ancient ruins, and exploring major cities and small towns. "So there I was," Tom remembered, "with all the liberty that I had been promising myself for so long. The world was mine. How did I like it? Instead of being filled with happiness and well-being, I was miserable."

He finally found contentment — and more — in Rome. This happened gradually. At first he reacted to the city much as he had when he had visited it before — he was not particularly impressed. But after about a week he began "looking into churches rather than into ruined temples." His initial interest in their Byzantine mosaics led him to "unconsciously and unintentionally [visit] all the great shrines of Rome." Soon, he found himself visiting them for their "interior peace" as well as their art. Their powerful Christian symbolism haunted him each evening when he returned to his hotel. He began reading the Bible again and visited the cathedrals more frequently. "I loved to be in these holy places," he remembered. "I had a kind

63

of deep and strong conviction that I belonged there: that my rational nature was filled with profound desires and needs that could only find satisfaction in churches of God."

One evening, as he was drifting off to sleep in his hotel room, Tom came to a sudden — and unexpected — realization that he desperately needed spiritual guidance, some assurance that life had a purpose beyond his own selfish needs:

It was night. The light was on. Suddenly it seemed to me that Father, who had now been dead more than a year, was there with me. The sense of his presence was . . . vivid and real. . . . The whole thing passed in a flash, but in that flash, instantly, I was overwhelmed with a sudden and profound insight into the mystery and corruption of my own soul . . . and I was filled with a horror of what I saw, and my whole being rose up in revolt against what was within me, and my soul desired escape and liberation from . . . all this with an intensity and an urgency unlike anything I had ever known before. And now I think for the first time in my whole life I really began to pray — praying not with my lips and my intellect and my imagination, but praying out of the very roots of my life and of my being . . . to the God I had never [really] known.

It would be several years until Tom was baptized as a Christian. As Tom himself acknowledged, "It would take me five or six years to discover what a frightful captivity I had got myself into." But this vision-like experience marked the beginning of a long spiritual journey, one that would eventually lead Thomas Merton to a Trappist monastery in Kentucky, nearly seven thousand miles away.

CHAPTER 7

The Reluctant Christian

The following day, Tom went into the church of Saint Sabina, "took holy water at the door and went straight up to the altar rail and knelt down and [prayed]." He had never done this before, and despite self-conscious feelings, he left feeling reborn. In his autobiography, Tom recalled that after he left the church, he sat in the sun and "turned over in my mind how my life was now going to change, and how I would become better." Now he became even more curious about Christian religious traditions and disciplines. He took a trolley from Rome to San Paolo, where a Trappist monastery overlooked the Tiber River. "I had no idea what Trappist monks were, or what they did, except that they kept silence," Tom remembered. He visited the old church adjoining the abbey, but he was afraid to venture inside the monastery itself.

Instead, he strolled around the peaceful grounds, enjoying the afternoon sun. During his walk, an unusual idea grew in his head: "I should like to become a Trappist monk," he thought. It was a fleeting notion, and he quickly put it aside. But the idea would return again and again over the course of the next eight years, gaining appeal each time it surfaced in Tom's thoughts. Eventually it would become a realistic goal, one that Tom would pursue with more enthusiasm and determinism than he could ever have imagined at the age of seventeen.

With the first semester at Cambridge still months away, Tom sailed from Genoa to New York to visit his brother and grandparents. John Paul was now a full-fledged teen, with friends and interests of his own. Although the brothers' affection for one another remained strong, they spent less time together than they had during the years before Tom went to Europe.

In Douglaston, Tom continued to read the Bible and tried to maintain his newfound habit of prayer, but he felt embarrassed at the prospect of being discovered at it: "I no longer dared to pray on my knees before going to sleep," he recalled. He went to Easter services at nearby Zion Episcopal Church, where his father had once been the organist. The minister's sermon left Tom uninspired, however, and he decided to try the Friends Meeting in Flushing, which his mother had sometimes attended. He felt comfortable in "the shared silence" of the Quaker congregation, but he was annoyed by the silly remarks made by a visitor, remarks that Tom felt interrupted the serenity of silent worship. "I went out of the meeting house saying to myself, 'They are like all the rest. In other churches it is the minister who hands out the commonplaces, and here it is liable to be just anybody.'"

Clearly, Tom's expectations for church worship were exceedingly high. He lacked the maturity to understand that worshipers of all the churches he visited were, like him, imperfect human beings, simply trying to express their devotion to God as best they could. Despite his recent vows of self-improvement, he was quick to point out the weaknesses of others, and he remained skeptical about organized religion.

And so, with the same impulsiveness with which he had adopted his goals of self-reform, he quickly dispensed with all hope of finding a religious denomination that suited him. Among family members, he became known as the "unmasker of religious hypocrisy," often arguing at mealtime with his Uncle Harold (his mother's younger brother) on subjects such as politics, individual freedom, and religion.

He made a brief trip to Chicago that summer, and when he returned, his "real but temporary religious fervor," as he described it, was essentially gone, and he became preoccupied with more earthly concerns. He spent many evenings that summer going to movies, prize fights, parties, burlesque shows, and local bars. He was frequently accompanied by Reginald Marsh, a bachelor artist and friend of Owen Merton's, who had a studio in Greenwich Village. Marsh was not a bad person, but Tom's grandparents did not approve of his bohemian lifestyle. Tom was now a manly eighteen, however, and the Jenkinses had little control over his behavior or his choice of friends. Marsh, like Tom Bennett, became a temporary role model. Night after night, Tom and Reginald went out on the town.

In September, Tom sailed back to England and began his university studies at Cambridge. He found it difficult, after his long summer of freedom, to settle down and focus his energies on academics. His grandparents were now an ocean away, and his godfather was busy practicing medicine in London. At a time when Tom needed emotional support and a strong male role model, he found himself with little adult supervision and no one to whom he was specifically accountable.

In November, his Aunt Maud died — an event that no doubt made him feel more alone than ever. "They buried my childhood with her," Tom wrote. "She . . . had presided in a certain sense over my most innocent days. And now I saw those days buried with her in the ground."

By now Tom had established some unhealthy habits — he smoked at least a pack of cigarettes a day and was a frequent patron of the local bars and pubs — which were costly in terms of time and money. Unlike Oakham, where there was little opportunity to mingle with members of the opposite sex, Cambridge provided Tom with many opportunities to meet young women.

The college itself had few female students, but Tom managed to meet several girls who lived in town and worked in the local shops, offices, and restaurants. Like many of the other students, he had his own apartment and could come and go as he pleased. He had frequent dates, and he was soon in trouble with his landlady for bringing girls to his flat late at night.

On weekends, he sometimes visited the Bennetts in London, but even there his behavior seemed to be out of control. He stayed out until very late at night, brought over some of his wilder friends, and dated girls who "were not the right kind." Finally, Iris Bennett told Tom that she had had enough of his self-centeredness and that she did not appreciate him and his friends "coming in at all hours, usually drunk and always noisy." From now on, when he came to London, he could stay in a hotel, she told him.

Tom Merton was clearly on a path of self-destruction. It seems, however, that he did not perceive the serious consequences of his delinquent behavior, nor did he feel inclined to stop it. He was having a good time, and for now that was all that mattered. He began receiving large bills for food, alcohol, tobacco, and stylish clothing. He stayed out late and slept until noon, often missing morning lectures. As a result, his grades suffered, and he was in danger of failing one of his classes.

Tom Bennett, who had become increasingly concerned over Tom's reckless behavior, finally summoned

Tom to his office. "The fifteen or twenty minutes that followed were among the most painful and distressing I have ever lived through," Tom wrote in his autobiography. "Not because of anything that he said to me, for he was not angry or even unkind. . . . The thing that made me suffer was that he asked me very bluntly and coldly for an explanation of my conduct and left me to writhe."

The confrontation left the teenager almost speechless, for he suddenly realized the extent to which he had disgraced himself and those who had trusted him to behave responsibly. "As soon as I was placed in the position of having to give some kind of . . . defence of so much stupidity and unpleasantness, . . . the whole bitterness and emptiness of it became very evident to me," he wrote. "The words I murmured about my 'making mistakes' and 'not wanting to hurt others' sounded extremely silly and cheap."

But even though the meeting made a powerful impression on Tom, his behavior didn't change. He remained self-indulgent and reckless. The loss of his beloved parents, a sense of rootlessness, the absence of a consistent role model, and his own emotional growing pains combined to produce in Tom Merton a potent recipe for disaster.

Unfortunately, Tom became friends with other first-year students at Cambridge whose behavior only reinforced his bad habits. Most of them enjoyed spending time in the pubs, flirting with girls in town, and attending parties in each other's rooms. And Tom drifted apart from friends like Andrew Winser, whom he had known at Oakham. Yet it was Andrew to whom Tom made a confession one day in the spring of 1934: he had apparently "got a girl into trouble"; he was "deeply distressed." This time, it seemed, he had gone too far.

In his autobiography, Tom didn't mention the fact that he fathered an out-of-wedlock child. Whether this was a purposeful omission or the result of censoring by his Catholic superiors remains a matter of speculation. Whatever the exact circumstances, it seems clear that "some legal settlement was made" at the time, according to biographer Michael Mott. His godfather apparently promised Tom that the Jenkins family wouldn't find out any details if the matter were kept out of court.

For Thomas Merton, life at Cambridge had consisted of a slow downward spiral, which suddenly accelerated to the point of chaos. Somehow, in the midst of these dreadful circumstances, he managed to finish the end-of-term exams (which he passed) and select a student apartment for the following academic year, thinking at that point that he would be returning.

With school over for the year, Tom sailed for New York, anxious to distance himself from the pain of recent months, from what he later referred to as his "experiments in being 'a man of the world.'" After arriving in Douglaston, he received a letter from Tom Bennett, informing him that his grades were not nearly good enough for him to continue on the career path he had chosen. Bennett went on to suggest that, in view of Tom's poor academic performance and his "mistakes in behavior," it would be better if he stayed in America. "It did not take me five minutes to come around to agreeing with him," Tom wrote in *The Seven Storey Mountain*. "The thought that I was no longer obliged to go back . . . filled me with an immense relief." But Tom's response to his godfather's letter may have been more complex than this remark indicates. In the letter, his godfather virtually disowned him, which must have been very painful.

In the fall, Tom made a brief trip to England to obtain the visa required for permanent residence in the United States. During the several weeks he was there, he saw Tom and Iris Bennett only once, and had no contact with any relatives; it's not clear how much time he spent with any of his friends. As soon as he had collected the necessary papers, he sailed back to New York. As he thought back on recent events, he was keenly reminded of the mistakes he had made: "A lot of things had happened to me since I had left the relative seclusion of Oakham, and had been free to indulge all my appetites in the world, and the time had come for a big readjustment in my values. I could not evade that truth. I was too miserable, and it was evident that there was too much wrong with my strange, vague, selfish hedonism."

When he returned to Douglaston, his grandparents and his Uncle Harold convinced him that he should finish his studies at an American university and obtain a degree. Tom chose Columbia University, a respected New York school located at the edge of that city's Harlem district. "Compared with Cambridge, this big sooty factory was full of light and fresh air," Tom wrote. "There was a kind of genuine intellectual vitality in the air . . . perhaps [because] most of the students had to work hard to pay for every classroom hour. . . . [And] therefore they appreciated what they got."

Tom began classes in January of 1935, and he felt comfortable there at once. The middle-class background of the students at Columbia created an environment that was more diverse, more friendly, and more tolerant than the sophisticated and sometimes snobbish atmosphere of Cambridge. His favorite class was Eighteenth-century Literature, taught by a young professor named Mark Van Doren. "Mark would come into the room and, without any fuss, start talking about whatever was to be talked about," Tom recalled. "Most of the time he asked questions . . . and if you tried to answer them intelligently, you found yourself saying excellent things that you did not know you knew, and that you had not, in fact, known before." Van Doren was to become a lifelong friend, and Tom continued to write to him after entering the monastery. Later, when Tom was teaching novice students there, he used Van Doren's lecture style.

After a few months at Columbia, Tom settled into a routine of attending classes, studying, writing, and working. He was aware that his godfather had rescued him from a shameful and embarrassing situation, and he was determined to take advantage of his second chance. He lived quietly with his grandparents in Douglaston (John Paul was attending a military academy in Gettysburg, Pennsylvania), and took the train to the campus each morning. He began reading books on Communism, and for a short time he was convinced that it offered a solution to the country's social problems. But this enthusiasm didn't last.

In the fall of 1935, when Tom started his next term at Columbia, he began to hit his stride. He signed up for an intriguing variety of classes, taking courses in Spanish, German, geology, constitutional law, and French Renaissance literature. He took up cross-country running and joined a fraternity. He also worked on the side, taking one part-time job as a foreign-language interpreter at the Rockefeller Center, another as a tutor, and a third drawing cartoons for a paper-cup manufacturer. In addition, he got involved with a number of the student-run publications at Columbia: he drew cartoons for *The Jester,* and wrote for *The Spectator, The Columbia Review,* and the yearbook.

His writing attracted the attention of Robert Giroux, who, along with another student, was editing the school's fine literary magazine, *The Columbia Review.* Robert and Tom became friends, and Tom began spending more time in John Jay Hall, where the offices of the magazine and other campus publications were located. And gradually, Tom met several other Columbia students who were to become his close personal friends. Seymour Freedgood, known as "Sy," and Robert Lax were roommates who shared Tom's interest in literature and his love of a good joke. Ed Rice was "a talented draftsman" whose humorous drawings frequently appeared beside Tom's in *The Jester*. Bob Gibney and Bob Gerdy completed this lively, literary-minded bunch. Their special interest in philosophy added insight and depth to the friends' many late-night conversations, which took place in Sy and Robert's cramped dormitory room. During these discussions, which frequently turned into debates, members of the group shared their views on politics, war, social justice, psychology, and religion.

But in spite of Tom's energy and enthusiasm and increasing self-confidence, his life was not quite as untroubled as it appeared to be on the surface. Besides being very active with school and extracurricular activities — perhaps hyperactive — Tom was also drinking and smoking heavily and going out to clubs frequently with his friends. And he had moments when he still thought that there was something very wrong with his life, when he felt empty and disgusted with himself.

Still, Tom was a popular figure on campus, and he was doing well in his studies and making a name for himself in student publications. By the end of the school year in the spring of 1936, he was the art editor of *The Jester* and continued to contribute to *The Spectator* and *The Columbia Review*.

But grief and loss were to enter Tom's life again. In late October of 1936, his grandfather suddenly fell ill and died. Tom was overcome by grief. He went into his grandfather's room and fell to his knees, "spontaneously praying beside [him]." Not long afterward, Bonnemaman also became ill, recovered, but then fell ill again and died the following summer. These twin losses were a crushing blow. "There had been too many deaths in Merton's young life," wrote biographer Monica Furlong. "Pop and Bonnemaman, from when he was six years old or so, had spelled the only domestic security he knew." Tom still had his Uncle Harold, but the two of them were not close, so Tom did not share his grief and confusion with him.

Tom kept up with the multiple demands of school and extracurricular activities, but he felt both anxious and depressed. Not surprisingly, his own health began to decline. He collapsed from exhaustion during a cross-country race and ended up quitting the team. He suffered from severe stomach pains, spells of dizziness, and insomnia. When he was returning to Columbia from Douglaston one day in November, he began to get vertigo on the train. Terrified, Merton got off at Penn Station, took a room at the Pennsylvania Hotel, and asked to see the house physician. The doctor who examined Tom in his hotel room told him that he was "overstimulated." The collapse was accompanied by stomach distress — the doctor thought he might even have an ulcer.

Tom suspected that his physical problems were partly the result of his psychological and spiritual depression. Since the night in Rome when he had imagined his father was beside him in the hotel room, he had been struggling to find a meaning for his life, for a way to make sense of the losses he had endured and the social injustices — poverty, crime, disease, war — that seemed to be gaining ground in the world. He had lost hope while at Cambridge; but at Columbia he had started to believe in himself again, and to wonder about God's role in his life. But he had also fallen back into the reckless, self-indulgent habits that had plagued his life at Cambridge.

Now he was at a crossroads in his spiritual journey. The loss of his grandparents had precipitated a physical, emotional, and spiritual crisis that he knew he must address if he was ever to have inner peace. He was suffering now from doubt, loneliness, fear, and despair, just as his father had suffered during his long illness. But his father had responded with renewed faith that had grown stronger during those final painful months. Now it seemed that God was calling Tom — could he also answer "yes" to faith?

As Tom struggled with his feelings of emptiness and despair, he realized that, until now, he had "tried to interpret life in terms of sociological and economic laws, but that these separated from faith and charity became yet another form of imprisonment." Once again, Thomas Merton felt trapped by the choices he had made; by asking for faith, he hoped he could begin again.

He spoke frequently about religion with his friends and with his favorite professor, Mark Van Doren. Tom's ideas on religion aligned most closely with those of Robert Lax, who seemed to have "an instinctive spirituality" and, according to Tom, "a mind full of tremendous and subtle intuitions." Lax, Seymour Freedgood, and Bob Gerdy were Jewish, Rice and Giroux were Catholic, and Gibney, like Tom, was uncommitted. As his friendship with these young men grew, however, Tom discovered that they were all "searching for some [meaningful] religious faith." He began to ask them questions about human spirituality and the need for religious affiliation.

Sy Freedgood introduced Tom to his friend Bramachari, a Hindu monk whose kindness, gentleness, and simplicity reminded Tom of the Privats in France. Bramachari was "a man profoundly centered on God," Tom remembered, who sensed Tom's spiritual longing and encouraged him to read *The Imitation of Christ* and Saint Augustine's *Confessions*. Tom was certainly surprised when the Hindu monk recommended these well-known Catholic books, but he took the monk's advice nonetheless. Tom also read *The Spirit of Medieval Philos-*

79

ophy by the French historian Étienne Gilson (1884-1978). Gilson's ideas finally "provided him with a concept of God that made intellectual sense to him." Through his reading of Catholic literature, both historical and contemporary, Tom gradually shed his prejudice against organized religion. He began to go to church again, sporadically attending the one he was most familiar with — the Zion Episcopal Church in Douglaston. He also felt "a growing desire to pray, and began to do so fairly regularly." He prayed for the courage to change, for the humility to seek God's direction for his life.

During the summer of 1938, his prayers were answered. One Sunday, instead of taking his usual trip to Long Island to see a girlfriend, he decided to go to Mass — for the first time. "The first time in my life!" Tom wrote. "That was true. I had lived for several years [in Europe], I had been to Rome, I had been in and out of a thousand Catholic cathedrals and churches, and yet I had never heard Mass. . . . I will not easily forget how I felt that day. There was this . . . urge in me which said, 'Go to Mass! Go to Mass!' It was something quite new and strange, this voice that seemed to prompt me."

He went to the Corpus Christi Church near Harlem. After the service began, Tom felt awkward and somewhat uncomfortable, because he was unfamiliar with the rituals, gestures, and prayers that made up the Catholic service. But he stayed and tried to follow along, listening attentively to the priest's sermon on the Incarnation. Afterward, he left the church filled with a kind of joy that was strange to him. "I could not understand what it was that had happened to make me so happy, why I was so much at peace, so content with life, for I was not yet used to the clean savor that comes with an actual grace. . . . All I know is that I walked in a new world."

He had been reading religious books at a rate that astounded his friends; now his reading "became more and more Catholic," he recalled. Having received his undergraduate degree from Columbia earlier that year, he had decided to pursue a master's degree in English and to write his thesis on the topic of nature and art in the work of William Blake. Blake's writing had first influenced Tom during his days at Oakham, but now he found the spiritual symbolism in Blake's poetry even more inspiring. Tom also read the work of Gerard Manley Hopkins, another British poet who converted to Catholicism and became a priest.

One evening, when Tom was reading about Hopkins' conversion, "the desire to take a similar step himself became irresistible." He paced back and forth in his apartment, then grabbed his coat and ran to the Corpus Christi Church. He found the priest, Father Ford, and blurted out, "I want to become a Catholic." The two talked for the rest of the evening, and Father Ford agreed that Tom should attend religious classes at the church.

For the next several weeks, Tom went to Corpus Christi to learn more about Catholic history, beliefs, and traditions. On November 16, 1938, he was baptized into the Catholic Church and received his first communion. "It had taken Merton a long while to move toward this decisive step, which was to change his whole life," wrote Monica Furlong. "After years of searching in many different places, he had found a home in the Church."

This is the "official portrait" of "Father Louis" taken by
John Howard Griffin in 1963. Tom's expression shows that
he was a monk but also a man engaged with the world.
Photograph copyright 1996 by Elizabeth Griffin-Bonazzi

Owen Merton and Ruth Merton. They were caring, creative parents, but Tom lost them both when he was young.

His mother died in 1921, when he was six; his father died in 1931, just before Tom turned sixteen.

(*Above*) Tom and John Paul together in Douglaston, New York
Courtesy of Abbey of Gethsemani Archives
(*Below*) Villa Diane, the home that Owen Merton built in St.
Antonin, France, several years after his wife's death. His plan
to live there with both of his sons never materialized.
Courtesy of the Thomas Merton Studies Center, Bellarmine College,
Copyright Trustees of the Merton Legacy Trust

The Lycée Ingres in Montauban, near St. Antonin, the
school Tom began attending when he was eleven.
He was often miserable there.

In 1929, a year after Tom's father took him to England,
Tom *(back row, third from left)* began attending
Oakham, a small college-prep academy.

Tom (far left) and his grandmother at the house in Douglaston in 1919. When Tom was 22, his grandparents died within a year of each other; he was devastated.

John Paul Merton (*right*) and a friend in uniform. When John Paul was killed in a plane crash in World War II, Tom wrote a moving poem as a tribute to him.

Tom *(left)* and Robert Lax in the editorial office
of *The Jester,* a Columbian student publication.
Tom began attending Columbia in 1935, after
his reckless year at Cambridge.
Columbian, Columbia College Yearbook, 1937.
Courtesy of Columbia University, Columbiana Collection

Mark Van Doren, who was Tom's favorite professor at Columbia.
Years later, after Tom had become "Father Louis" at
Gethsemani, he adopted Van Doren's teaching style
when he instructed young monks.
Courtesy of the Thomas Merton Studies Center, Bellarmine College,
Copyright Trustees of the Merton Legacy Trust

Corpus Christi Church in New York City, where Tom was baptized
on November 16, 1938. This was the first of several
spiritual turning points in Tom's life.
Courtesy of Corpus Christi Church

Another turning point: After he was rebuffed as an applicant to
the Franciscan Order, Tom *(third from left)* became
a teacher at St. Bonaventure College.
Courtesy of the Thomas Merton Studies Center, Bellarmine College,
Copyright Trustees of the Merton Legacy Trust

Perhaps the biggest turning point in Tom's life: the day he entered
Gethsemani monastery for a week's retreat. Less than a year later,
on December 10, 1941, he returned for a lifetime.

The ordination of Thomas Merton *(far right)* as a priest on May 26, 1949. By this time, Tom, the "writing monk" of Gethsemani, had published several books, including *The Seven Storey Mountain*.

Several of Tom's friends attended the ordination ceremonies. Pictured from left to right are Seymour Freedgood, Robert Giroux, James Laughlin, Dan Walsh, Robert Lax, and Ed Rice.

Naomi Burton, Tom's literary agent. She represented him in 1946, when she sent the manuscript of *The Seven Storey Mountain* to Robert Giroux at Harcourt, Brace.

Young monks gathered for study *(above)*, and *(below)* Tom *(front row, center)* photographed with one of his classes of young monks. Even though the teaching he did as Master of Scholastics (and, later, Master of Novices) made him extremely busy, he enjoyed it. "Teaching knocks me out," he wrote to a friend.
Both photos courtesy of Abbey of Gethsemani Archives

An exterior shot of the hermitage and its surrounding woods, which Tom wrote about in vivid detail.

Tom in the sparsely furnished hermitage. He was allowed to live there full-time in August of 1965.
Photograph by John Howard Griffin, copyright 1996 by Elizabeth Griffin-Bonazzi

Tom saying Mass at Gethsemani in 1966. On this occasion he had several visitors, including the French philosopher Jacques Maritain and Tom's first mentor, Father Dan Walsh.

"Father Louis" in denim, 1967. The camera around Tom's neck was on "perpetual loan" from a friend.

Tom had been interested in Eastern philosophy and religion for years, so his meetings with the Dalai Lama in Dharamsala, Tibet, were one of the highlights of his trip to Asia in 1968.

Tom at the conference of monastic leaders in Bangkok in December of 1968. The conference began on December 9; Tom died on December 10.

The simple marker on Tom's grave in the Gethsemani cemetery. He
left behind a rich legacy of writing, teaching, faith, and friendship.

CHAPTER 8

Home, at Last

On February 22, 1939, Columbia University awarded Tom a Master of Arts degree in English literature. In the course of pursuing his M.A., Tom had become close friends with Dan Walsh, a religion professor who was visiting from Sacred Heart College in Manhattan. Dan and Tom had frequent discussions about religion and, in particular, what it meant to be a Catholic in modern times. Dan perceived that Tom's interest in religious philosophy was deeper than that of most students and wondered if he had a "calling" to the religious life.

As their friendship grew, Tom admitted that he was curious about religious vocations; sometimes he even imagined himself a priest. He and Dan talked at great length about the different Catholic orders (separate communities of Christian men and women who devote much of their lives to prayer and meditation) that existed in the United States. Tom asked about the Benedictines, the Jesuits, the Dominicans, the Franciscans, and the Cistercians (or Trappists), and he learned that each order had its own unique requirements for behavior, dress, worship, and diet. Some orders were more strict than others, but all of them required members to give up their worldly possessions, to devote several hours each day to prayer and meditation, and to live in a community with other like-minded individuals (who were referred to as "brothers" or "sisters"). These requirements were designed to free them from secular distractions, thereby fostering a close relationship with God.

Tom considered each order carefully, weighing the advantages and disadvantages of each. He liked the Dominicans, but was "put off" by the fact that they slept in a dormitory. The life of the Benedictines was also attractive, but he was afraid of "ending up as a schoolmaster," and the Jesuits "seemed altogether too busy and worldly." The Franciscans were most appealing because their life was less structured, and they were committed to "the ideal of poverty."

At first, the idea of joining a religious order — and leaving the comforts and freedoms to which he'd grown accustomed — seemed interesting but improbable and even somewhat frightening to Tom. But gradually, and for reasons that Tom did not initially understand, he began to consider the religious life more seriously. In quiet moments, when he was having breakfast at the nearby German bakery, or lying awake at night in his apartment, or browsing through the book stacks at the public library, he would suddenly think, "I am going to be a priest." When he shared this thought with a few of his friends, however, they quickly passed it off as "one of [Tom's] sudden enthusiasms."

In September of 1939, England declared war on Germany. The thought of another world war (Tom's parents had fled Europe during the first one) was almost too much for Tom to bear. Why was it, he wondered, that people couldn't settle their differences in a nonviolent manner? Why should innocent people lose their lives and their loved ones for the sake of political boundaries or cultural differences? These were questions that troubled him deeply, questions that he would ponder in greater depth in the decades to come. There were also more immediate and personal reasons for his concern: Tom and his college friends were all eligible for the draft (obligatory military service), and John Paul, a recent graduate of military school, would most certainly be called to fight.

Tom wasn't sure how much religious beliefs should affect politics, but he guessed that they were, in some ways, related. Since his baptism, he had become more concerned about the realities of war, poverty, prejudice, crime, and other social problems. But being concerned, he felt, was not enough; social problems required not only understanding but action. So he began volunteering at Friendship House, a homeless shelter in Harlem. He prepared hot meals, sorted clothing to be distributed among the poor, and entertained children of destitute families. Those who knew him said that Tom's concern for the poor was "deep and sincere."

Earlier in the year, Tom had moved into a new apartment on Perry Street in Greenwich Village, a section of New York City that was popular among writers, painters, and playwrights. This was a busy and intellectually demanding time: besides working on his Ph.D., he was also writing book reviews for the *New York Times* and the *Herald Tribune,* as well as spending some nights teaching extension courses in English literature at Columbia University. He had completed the manuscript of his first novel, "The Labyrinth" (which was heavily autobiographical), and was hard at work on another, "The Man in the Sycamore Tree." The main character of the second book is a young man named Jim Mariner who grows increasingly disillusioned with life and falls into despair. He considers becoming a priest in order to free himself from a world on the edge of disaster.

Like many writers, Tom attempted to sort out issues and conflicts in his own life by assigning them to a fictitious character. At one point, the character Jim considers the pleasures he will forsake if he chooses to become a priest: "He would never go dancing again, and there would be no more parties. . . . He would never be able to hitch hike, if he felt like it, to California, or move wherever he pleased," Tom wrote. Through

Jim Mariner, Tom was able to explore his own fears about leaving the secular world and entering a religious community.

As the weeks passed, Tom became more and more convinced that he could give up parties, loud music, dancing, and dating girls. But there *was* one aspect of his life that he wished he could retain. Since his boyhood days in France — when he had walked with his school chums through the countryside, and they had discussed the plots of each other's books — Tom had dreamed of becoming a writer. Through his reading and his discussions with Dan Walsh, Tom knew that most religious orders required members to follow a strict schedule of work, rest, and prayer. Such a prescribed lifestyle would leave little time for creative expression, he imagined. If joining a religious order would mean giving up his dream of becoming a writer, would it be too high a price to pay?

The question haunted him day and night, for he was now spending almost all of his free time writing. In addition to writing novels and book reviews, he was also keeping a daily journal and writing poems. His previous attempts at poetry had been unsuccessful because he had lacked the emotional honesty that the form required. Since his conversion, however, he had worked hard to uncover and understand some of the negative feelings — guilt, self-doubt, anger, shame — that had caused much of his self-destructive behavior. As a result of his increasing self-awareness, his writing

87

became more personal, his images deeper and more interesting.

Tom now began to test his readiness to enter a religious order by making conscious sacrifices in several areas. He gave up cigarettes entirely, rarely indulged in alcohol, limited his spending, and dated girls only occasionally. This last change seemed a bit drastic to his friends, but since it was the hardest to accomplish, it gave him the greatest sense of peace.

The time that he had previously spent indulging in these habits he now spent reading, writing, and praying. He began going to Mass every day, and to memorize many of the traditional Catholic prayers. "[He] still very much wanted to lead a life of dedication to God," wrote biographer Monica Furlong; "indeed, he knew that he must, if he was not to destroy himself with his appetites, as had nearly happened in the past."

In October of 1939, Dan Walsh introduced Tom to a priest at the Franciscan house on 31st Street in New York. Tom was "warmly received" there, "questioned about his vocation [his Divine calling], and told that he might make an application to be received the following August." Tom was overjoyed at the offer, but disappointed that he would have to wait so long for word of his acceptance. The priest remained firm, however: the Franciscans took in new members (called novices) only once each year, and they didn't make exceptions.

So Tom decided, wisely, to use the intervening months to write, teach, and strive to develop the emotional and spiritual discipline that he would need to live as a Franciscan. He prayed often, continued to attend Mass daily, and began reading a copy of *The Spiritual Exercises of St. Ignatius* (originally designed to train Jesuit priests), which "he proceeded to go through . . . an hour at a time, sitting cross-legged on the floor" of his apartment on Perry Street.

In April of 1940, he became suddenly ill and underwent an operation to remove his appendix. After a brief stay in the hospital, he went to his Uncle Henry's house in Douglaston to rest. This period of convalescence allowed him to read, to meditate, and to pray.

Once he was fully recovered, he took a vacation to Cuba, traveling alone and staying in cheap hotels and enjoying the numerous churches within walking distance of where he was staying. In these churches "there were a thousand things to do, a thousand ways of easily making a thanksgiving," Tom wrote. "Everything lent itself to Communion: I could hear another Mass, I could say the Rosary, do the Stations of the Cross, or if I just knelt where I was, everywhere I turned my eyes I saw saints in wood or plaster or those who seemed to be saints in flesh and blood." The island's natural beauty impressed him, but he was most impressed by the intense Christian devotion of its people: in the many churches he visited, he saw Cubans in prayer "everywhere." Even though Tom was on vacation, his trip became a kind of spiritual pilgrimage, he recalled, because he "was learning a thing that could not be completely learned except in a culture that is at least outwardly Catholic. One needs the atmosphere of French or Spanish or Italian Catholicism before there is any possibility of a complete and total experience of all the natural and sensible joys that overflow from the Sacramental life." And just as the European culture had inspired his father's drawing and painting, the Cuban culture inspired Tom's poetry, as an excerpt from one of his early poems shows:

Five angels beating bongos,
Seven saints ringing their bells,
Wear coats made out of paper money
And shoes made out of shells.

When Tom returned to New York in May, only three months remained until he would join the Franciscans. They had sent word that his application and personal recommendations were in order, and it seemed likely that he would be accepted in August.

While he waited for official notice, he rented out his apartment on Perry Street and joined his Columbia friends at a rural cottage near Olean, New York. (Tom had been there briefly the summer before.) Sy Freedgood's sister, Gladys, and her husband owned the house, but they allowed Sy and his Columbia friends to use it during the summer. Ed Rice, Bob Gerdy, Bob Gibney, Robert Lax, and Ad Reinhardt were all staying with Sy and Tom at the cottage, which soon became "impossibly crowded" and

terribly noisy. "There is always someone eating . . ., someone sleeping, someone cooking, someone typing, drawing, chopping wood, rattling dishes, pouring coffee,"
wrote Tom's friend Ed Rice. Tom remembered eating
waffles or hamburgers for nearly every meal, playing
Cuban bongo drums on the porch, and erecting a make-
shift trapeze in the front yard.

The cottage provided an escape from the confines of
the city, and gave the young men a chance to enjoy
some recreation and to renew their close friendships.
But Tom soon found himself longing for a little privacy,
peace, and quiet. He arranged to stay in a dormitory at
St. Bonaventure's, a Catholic college in Olean that was
run by the Franciscan fathers. He spent two peaceful
weeks there performing simple tasks. He scrubbed
floors, washed dishes, worked in the garden — and
fantasized about his future life as a Franciscan. Because
of the way he had lived his life for the past several years,
the quiet life of prayer seemed attractive. He even day-
dreamed about having a new name; "Frater John Spani-
ard" came to mind.

But after he returned to the cottage, Tom was suddenly overcome by doubts about his worthiness to join
the Franciscans. Although he had confessed his past
sins (drinking, overspending, and the affair that had
produced an out-of-wedlock child) at his first confession, he had not mentioned these transgressions during
the interview for admittance into the order. When his
friends began discussing their obligation to serve in the

military (the Germans invaded France in June of 1940, forcing the United States to reconsider its neutral stance), Tom was further confused. Ever since the war had begun in Europe, he had "wrestl[ed] with . . . his own inner bafflement that there are people in the world who want war, usually because they want something other people have." Now he wondered if his urgent calling to the Franciscan order was partly, if unconsciously, motivated by his hatred of violence and his desire to avoid the draft.

Whatever the reasons for his sudden wave of self-doubt, Tom could not rest until he confessed his earlier transgressions to the Franciscans. He took the train from Olean back to the city, "hoping a little that his own doubts and fears might be waved aside." He then arranged a hurried meeting with the priest who had taken his application and confessed his troubles at Cambridge and his affair with the English girl. But what he had hoped for did not happen. The Franciscans took "a serious view" of Tom's past life, and when the priest met with Tom again a few days later, he recommended that Tom withdraw his application. Dazed, Tom went to a nearby church and entered a confessional. He tried to explain what was troubling him, but the priest misunderstood, and even ended up saying that Tom "certainly did not belong in the monastery, still less the priesthood." Understandably, this deepened Tom's distress. "When I came out of that ordeal, I was completely broken in pieces," Tom wrote. "I could not keep back the tears, which ran down between the fingers of the hands in which I concealed my face. . . . The only thing I knew, besides my own tremendous misery, was that I must no longer consider that I had a vocation to the cloister."

Tom returned to Olean and faced the awful task of explaining his rejection to his friends. Although he was devastated, he maintained the conviction that God intended him to lead a spiritual life. "If I could not be a religious, a priest — that was God's affair," he wrote. "But nevertheless He still wanted me to lead something of the life of a priest or of a religious." In fact, Tom had announced to the priest who told him to reconsider his vocation, " 'I am going to try to live like a religious.' "

He decided to join the Third Order of Franciscans at St. Bonaventure's College. This lay (non-priestly) order afforded him the chance to remain in the secular world while developing a meaningful connection with the Franciscans. He wore a scapular (two pieces of cloth joined by a string at the shoulders) under his regular clothes and said the office (prescribed prayers) every day, just as an ordained priest might do.

Around this same time, he applied for and got a job teaching English at St. Bonaventure's. "I moved into the little room that was assigned to me on the second floor of the big, red-brick building that was both a dormitory and a monastery," he wrote. "Out of my window I could look beyond the chapel front to the garden and fields and the woods. . . . My eyes often wandered out there, and rested in that peaceful scene, and the landscape became associated with my prayers."

His days were challenging and full. He taught three classes of thirty students each, prepared lectures, corrected papers, held office hours, and administered exams. He also kept track of the manuscript of his first novel, "The Labyrinth," which was still circulating among New York publishers. In the little spare time that remained, he wrote poetry and took long walks through the countryside, repeating passages from the breviary (the book of daily prayers) and asking God for world peace.

Despite his most fervent prayers, the war in Europe continued to escalate, and the United States was slowly being drawn into it. In November of 1940, Tom and his colleagues were summoned to one of the lecture halls, where they gave their names to the draft board. "I gave my name and my age and all the rest, and got a small white card," Tom remembered. "It was enough to remind me that I was not going to enjoy this pleasant and safe and stable life forever."

An official from the draft board told Tom that he would soon be required to take a medical exam, and if he passed, he would be eligible for active military service. In the meantime, he could continue his teaching at St. Bonaventure's. But Tom had already decided that he would not fight; instead, he would ask to be classified as a "non-combatant objector." This would allow him to serve in the medical corps as a hospital orderly or stretcher-bearer, but he would not have to carry a gun. Tom would serve "so long as I did not have to drop bombs on open cities, or shoot at other men," he wrote. "After all, Christ did say: 'Whatsoever you have done to the least of these my brethren, you did it to me.'"

His brother, John Paul, held a different view. When he visited Tom that winter, he told Tom that he had joined the naval reserve but had had "some differences of opinion" with his commanding officers. He was now hoping to join another military group, and was considering the Royal Canadian Air Force.

In January of 1941, Tom turned twenty-six. The peaceful calm of the snow-covered campus inspired him, and toward the beginning of Lent he experienced a sudden burst of creativity in his writing. He had been reading the work of Spanish poet Garcia Lorca, whom he greatly admired, and had begun fasting for Lent. The two practices combined, he recalled, to "let loose the string of my tongue," and he produced a number of good poems, which he promptly sent out to magazine publishers.

He kept in touch with his friends from Columbia, especially Ed Rice, Robert Lax, and Dan Walsh. Dan had recently returned from Kentucky, where he made his annual retreat to the Trappist monastery of Gethsemani. He had spent a week there praying, meditating, and taking part in the services and rituals performed by the resident fathers. Tom remembered from an earlier conversation with Dan that the Trappists were a strict order. Members remained within the walls of the monastery, obeyed the abbot, participated in long daily sessions of group prayer (they woke at two in the morning for the first one), fasted frequently, and performed hard physical labor. They lived in "cells," small rooms that were sparsely furnished, and were permitted to speak only during church services and when addressing the abbot. (They used a special sign language to communicate among themselves.) Contact with the outside world was extremely limited: members were allowed to write only two letters per year.

When Dan had first told Tom about Gethsemani, Tom had been both intrigued and perplexed by it. He believed that personal sacrifice brought spiritual healing, but the Trappist lifestyle seemed a bit severe nevertheless. Trappists were also known as "the Cistercians of the Strict Observance" — and "the very title made me shiver," Tom recalled. At the time he hadn't been sure he could endure the physical hardships — the cold, the manual labor, the fasting, the limited sleep — even for a week: "My mind was full of misgivings about [frequent] fasting and enclosure and all the long prayers and community life and monastic obedience and poverty, and there were plenty of strange spectres dancing about in the doors of my imagination, all ready to come in, if I would let them in. And if I did, they would show me how I would go insane in a monastery, and how my health would crack up, and my heart would give out, and I would collapse and go to pieces and be cast back into the world a hopeless moral and physical wreck."

Despite these misgivings, Tom had remained curious about the Trappists. And shortly before spring came to Saint Bonaventure's, he began thinking that he wanted to make a retreat in a monastery for Holy Week and Easter. And "the first place that came into my mind," he wrote, "was the Trappist abbey Dan Walsh had told me about, in Kentucky." What accounted for this about-face? "Something had opened out, inside me, in the last months," he wrote, "something that required, demanded at least a week in that silence, in that austerity, praying together with the monks in their cold choir." At the St. Bonaventure library, he looked up the Cistercian Order (and others) in the Catholic Encyclopedia. "What I saw on those pages pierced me to the heart like a knife," he later wrote in *The Seven Storey Mountain*. "[These men] were poor, they had nothing, and therefore they were free and possessed everything. . . . They worked with their hands . . . and everything around them was simple and primitive and poor. . . . Above all, they had found Christ. . . . And the love of Christ overflowing in those clean hearts made them children and made them eternal."

Tom wrote a letter to Gethsemani and asked for permission to make a retreat there in the spring. In late March he received a reply, telling him that he was welcome to come during Easter week. A few days later, Tom received another letter, this time from the draft board, telling him to report to a doctor's office in Olean for a medical exam. The war was inching ever closer to the peacefulness of St. Bonaventure's.

Tom accepted the invitation to Gethsemani and reported to the doctor's office for his exam. The physician in charge checked Tom's height and weight, tested his reflexes, took a sample of his blood, looked at his feet, and checked his teeth. (Over the years, Tom had had several infected teeth pulled.) When the exam was finished, Tom asked, "What about it, Doc?" The doctor replied, "Oh, go home. You haven't got enough teeth [to pass the physical]." For the time being, at least, it seemed that Tom was safe from the military.

The week before Easter found Tom correcting exams and preparing for his retreat. When school was out, he took a train from New York to Cincinnati, Ohio, then another to Louisville and went on to Bardstown, Kentucky, where Gethsemani was located. He arrived a little after eight in the evening on Palm Sunday to find the monastery completely dark. The man that drove him out to the monastery had told him that the monks went to bed by seven. The monk who let Tom in the front gate asked him several whispered questions, then asked, "Have you come here to stay?" Tom was shocked by the question. "The question terrified me," Tom recalled. "It sounded too much like the voice of my own conscience." His reply was "Oh, no!" followed by his "lame" explanation that he had a job. The monk nodded and led him down a dark hallway, up four flights of stairs, and into a large room. Except for a bed and a large wooden cross on the wall, the room was totally empty.

Tom slept for a few hours but was awakened at four A.M. by a bell, signalling an end to the "night office," the community prayer, and the beginning of Mass. Though exhausted from the trip, Tom didn't want to miss his first opportunity for worship: "I groped half blind with sleep for my clothing, and hastened into the hall and down the dark stairs," he remembered. In his autobiography, he recorded his impressions of that first night:

> The cloister was cold, and dimly lit, and the smell of damp wool [the monks wore heavy wool robes] astounded me by its unearthliness. . . . I stepped into the cloister as if into an abyss. The silence with people moving in it was ten times more gripping than it had been in my own empty room. . . . How did I live through the next hour? It is a mystery to me. The silence, the solemnity, the dignity of these Masses and of the church, and the overpowering atmosphere of prayers so fervent that they were almost tangible choked me with love and reverence that robbed me of the power to breathe. I could only get the air in gasps.

Kneeling down in church with these long-robed, silent men, Tom was struck by the realization that the Trappists were sacrificing their whole lives, as Christ had sacrificed his, for the rest of the world. He felt as if Christ was there with him, saying, "These men are dying for Me. These monks are killing themselves for Me: and for you, for the world, for the people who do not know Me, for the millions who will never know them on this earth."

As the days passed, Tom's admiration for the austere but God-centered life of the Trappists increased. He noticed one man in particular, a postulant (a candidate who has not yet been officially accepted) who, unlike Tom, hoped to stay at Gethsemani permanently: "[He was] a young man with black hair, in a pair of dungarees," Tom recalled. "For a couple of days . . . practically the first thing you noticed, when when you looked at the choir, was this young man in secular clothes, among all the monks. Then suddenly, we saw him no more. He was in white . . . and you could not pick him out from the rest. . . . The waters had closed over his head, and he was submerged in the community. . . . He had drowned to our society and become a Cistercian."

Tom's admiration for this community triggered a struggle inside him. He still had an "intense desire" to join a religious community, but he also knew that his "old scars [his rejection by the Franciscans] had not yet healed." When the retreat ended, Tom returned to Saint Bonaventure's full of awe and respect for the Trappists. But the struggle still raged inside him. Could he again open himself to the possibility of rejection by confessing all to the Trappists? Would their reaction be different from that of the Franciscans? If he applied, would they also take "a serious view" of his past life and reject him?

For the next several months, Tom asked himself these questions over and over again. His fear of rejection remained strong. At the same time, however, he felt homesick for Gethsemani. In the short time he had spent there, he had experienced a strong sense of belonging, as if the monastery were the home he had been searching for all along.

That summer he continued to examine and try to define his calling. He made a retreat to another Trappist monastery — Our Lady of the Valley in Rhode Island — and he also worked for Friendship House, the homeless shelter in Harlem where he had volunteered before.

He could not yet bring himself to seek admittance as a postulant to Gethsemani. But he knew that he wanted to give his whole life to God, and he decided that by dedicating himself to serving others who were less fortunate, he could accomplish this. He began to feel the need to leave St. Bonaventure's. "I did not belong there any more," he wrote in *The Seven Storey Mountain*. "It was too tame, too safe, too sheltered. It demanded nothing of me. It had no particular cross."

In the fall of 1941, he went to the office of the president at St. Bonaventure's and resigned his post as professor of English. "I'm going to Harlem," he announced to Father Thomas. At the beginning of 1942, Tom told the father, he planned to live permanently at Friendship House. There he would devote his talents to serving those who were poor and in despair.

Father Thomas agreed that this seemed a worthy

vocation, but wondered if it was the *right* vocation for Tom: What about becoming a priest? he asked. Tom replied, "I have thought about it, Father. But I don't believe I have that vocation." When he met with his friend Mark Van Doren during the Thanksgiving holiday, Tom heard the question again: "What about your idea of being a priest? Did you ever take that up again?"

The repeated question — and increasing doubts about whether going to Friendship House was the right thing to do — made Tom struggle toward an answer in a new way. Several days later, an answer came in the form of "a vivid conviction": "The time has come for me to go and be a Trappist," he thought. He tried to push the thought out of his mind by going to the dining hall for supper. But when he returned to his room, he discovered that the conviction was as strong as ever. He felt an urgency to talk to someone who could confirm his conviction, someone who could assure him that his past doubts could now be overcome. He decided to seek out Father Philotheus, a priest whom Tom had met during his first weeks at St. Bonaventure. Tom had come to know him as "a wise and good philosopher" whom he could trust "with the most involved spiritual problem." But when he got downstairs and went within several feet of the father's door, he lost his nerve and ran out into the courtyard. "I don't think there was ever a moment in my life when my soul felt so urgent and so special an anguish," he wrote in *The Seven Storey*

Mountain. In a quiet grove of trees nearby, he knelt before a little shrine of Thérèse of Lisieux, Tom prayed to the saint for guidance, asking her to give him a sign that he should enter the monastery. "As soon as I had made that prayer," Tom recalled, ". . . in my imagination, I started to hear the great bell of Gethsemani ringing in the night . . . as if it were just behind the first hill. . . . The bell seemed to be telling me where I belonged — as if it were calling me home."

Now Tom was determined to talk to Father Philotheus — but the light in the window of his room had gone out. Still determined, Tom ventured into the Friars' common room (a room he had never dared enter before), and happened to find the priest there. After the two went to Father Philotheus's room, Tom told the priest everything about his past life and his doubts about his vocation to the monastery. When he finished, Father Philotheus said that he saw no reason why Tom shouldn't be a priest. He had only one question for him: "Are you sure you want to be a *Trappist*?!" Tom nodded: "I want to give God everything."

That night was a turning point in Tom's life. He wrote to the abbot of Gethsemani, asking permission to make a retreat there in late December and "trying to hint that he really wanted to come as a postulant." The reply came quickly: yes, Tom could come at Christmastime. A few days later, he received another letter from the draft board, asking him to appear for a second physical exam. The requirements for enlistment had been "tightened up," so in all probability, bad teeth or not, Tom would soon be called to military service. He wrote to the draft board immediately and asked for a delay, explaining that he might soon be admitted to a monastery. At the end of that week — on December 7, 1941 — Japan bombed Pearl Harbor, and the United States went to war. The very next day, this grim news was followed by good news for Tom from the draft board: his medical exam was put off until mid-January. There was no time to lose.

He went to Father Thomas, explained his situation, and asked for permission to leave immediately. Even though he was still uncertain about his permanent acceptance by Gethsemani, he parted with most of his things. He packed just one suitcase full of personal belongings; he put most of his clothes in a box for Friendship House, and he gave away most of his books. He sent what was called "the Cuban journal" to the woman who ran Friendship House. He sent his poems and his journals and the manuscript of one novel to Mark Van Doren, asking him to keep them secure while he sorted out his vocation. (Years later, after Tom was an established writer, much of this work was published.) He burned the other manuscripts of his novels (a painful act for any writer), and sent what was left of his writing to Robert Lax and Ed Rice. He wrote farewells to them as well as to John Paul and his Uncle Harold in Douglaston.

On Tuesday evening, December 9, Tom boarded the

southbound train in Olean. "[I felt] an amazing and joyous sense of lightness," he wrote. "[When] I got on, . . . my last tie with the world I had known snapped and broke. . . . This journey, this transition from the world to a new life, was like flying through some strange new element — as if I were in the stratosphere. And yet I was on the familiar earth."

Tom took one train to Cincinnati, then another to Louisville, where he boarded a bus to Bardstown, near Gethsemani. The sun was up when he reached the monastery, and though he was tired from the long journey, he felt calm, happy, and at peace. Brother Matthew, who Tom remembered from his Easter retreat, met him at the gate. Seeing Tom's suitcase, he asked if Tom had come this time to stay. "Yes, Brother, if you'll pray for me," Tom replied. Brother Matthew smiled. "That's what I've been doing," he said.

Thomas Merton was home at last.

CHAPTER 9

Inside the Walls

When he left the secular world and entered Gethsemani, Tom had to make some radical changes. The Trappist way of life had changed little in its six-hundred-year history. The principles of simplicity, sacrifice, penance, and obedience remained at its core, and the rituals supporting them were still deeply rooted in medieval tradition.

Tom was received as a postulant three days after he arrived. For the first two days he stayed in the guesthouse and was put to work washing dishes and polishing floors. He received visits from the Master of Novices, whose job it was to determine "the sincerity of his intention." During one of these visits, Tom confessed everything about his past, including his affair at Cambridge. "He did not seem to be disturbed," Tom recalled. "He just said that he liked the way I had told him all that there was to be told, and that he would consult Father Abbot about it." Tom

106

was half-expecting to be "cross-examined" by the Abbot, but instead he was admitted as a postulant without reservation.

From that moment on, he was required to participate in the daily routine of worship, work, meals, and rest, and he was subject to the rules and regulations of the order. Nearly every activity of a monk's day was prescribed, so when a postulant entered Gethsemani, he necessarily sacrificed hobbies and other leisure activities. The day began at two A.M., when the monks rose for the "night office." This was followed by "mental prayer, Angelus [devotional prayer accompanied by bells], and private masses, said simultaneously at the side altars." Additional prayer times, worship services, and pious readings were scheduled in the choir throughout the rest of the day; meals, physical labor (mostly in the fields, orchards, and barns of Gethsemani's large working farm), and sleep filled the remaining hours. "It was a wonderful life if you could stand it," said John Eudes Bamberger, a monk who was at Gethsemani with Tom. "The silence tended to make it very intense. And there weren't too many emotional outlets. But it had as its rationale that one had to discover inner ways, the inner path, and discover the inner light, and focus on creating a life where emotions were increasingly invested in your relationship with the Lord in prayer. And once you caught on to that, gradually it seemed less and less austere."

In the beginning at least, Tom found this rigid lifestyle a refreshing change. In the modern secular world, the burden of constant choice — what to wear, eat, and buy, where to live, what career to pursue, whether to marry or remain single — seemed to rob even the most virtuous individuals of precious time and energy. As a postulant at Gethsemani, however, Tom had those decisions made for him — all he had to do was accept them.

During his first weeks there, Tom was infatuated with the Trappist lifestyle, and he behaved like a man who had just fallen in love. He devoted himself completely to learning the daily routine, the complicated sign language (the only acceptable form of communication), the order of worship and prayer during Mass, and the duties he was expected to perform in the monastery. It was a whole new way of life, one which — for a recently converted Catholic — must have taken an enormous amount of energy. But Tom embraced it willingly and enthusiastically because he believed it was God's will. In *The Seven Storey Mountain,* he wrote,

> The monastery is a school — a school in which we learn from God how to be happy. Our happiness consists in sharing the happiness of God, the perfection of His unlimited freedom, the perfection of His love. . . .
>
> The beginning of love is truth, and before He will give us His love, God must cleanse our souls of the lies that are in them. And the most effective way of detaching us from ourselves is to make us detest ourselves as

we have made ourselves by sin, in order that we may love Him reflected in our souls as He has re-made them by His love.

That is the meaning of the contemplative life, and the sense of all the apparently meaningless little rules and observances and fasts and obediences and penances and humiliations and labors that go to make up the routine of existence in a contemplative monastery: they all serve to remind us of what we are and Who God is — that we may get sick of the sight of ourselves and turn to Him: and in the end, we will find Him in ourselves, our own purified natures. . . .

Indeed, becoming sick of oneself was something that Tom had experienced repeatedly in his youth. At Gethsemani, he hoped that by "losing himself" — his ambitions, his secular identity, his painful past — he could be remade and reborn in the spirit of Christ. It was a challenging goal, one that he would spend the rest of his life achieving.

In February of 1942, Tom was officially accepted into the order as a novice, the first stage in his official consecration as a Trappist. "When you enter a Cistercian monastery," Tom wrote in *The Sign of Jonas*, "you spend some time as a postulant. After that you are a novice for two years, during which you hope to learn the rudiments of the Trappist life and discover whether or not you belong in the monastery. After that you make temporary simple vows for three years. These serve to prolong your probation [waiting period]. If, after these five years of probation, you want to leave, you are free to do so. If you stay, you make solemn perpetual vows. By these vows you consecrate your whole life to God in the monastery. After that you just forget about going back to the world."

Upon beginning his novitiate (the period of training as a novice), Tom was given the title "Frater [Brother] Louis." The name brought back memories of the day he sailed for Europe with his father — on The Feast of St. Louis of France — when he was just ten years old. "That sailing was a grace," Tom wrote in his autobiography. "Perhaps ultimately my vocation goes back to the days I spent in France, if it goes back to anything in the natural order."

At the monastery's tailor shop, Tom exchanged his street clothes for the traditional monk's habit. In winter, this consisted of a long woolen robe, a scapular, and a cowl (hood), which all together weighed about twenty pounds. Underneath he wore a long denim shirt, a pair of leggings made of duck cloth (tightly woven linen or cotton fabric), heavy socks, and a single pair of oversize shoes (to accommodate the socks). Like the Amish, the Trappists believed that buttons were "sinfully modern," so they tied their clothes together using cord or strips of soft cloth.

The tailor told Tom that he would receive freshly laundered underclothes every two weeks, and fresh outer garments every four. He was also given a set of work clothes — reinforced boots and a robe-like denim shirt that was to be worn over the habit in winter and in place of it in summer. He was expected to sleep in his robe (there was no heat in the dormitory) and to keep it reasonably clean for a month. Summer clothes, which were distributed around Easter, were lighter, but as biographer Michael Mott pointed out, "they must have been cruelly hot in Kentucky in July and August."

Mealtime provided another major change. During his college years, Tom had frequently eaten alone in his apartment or with a small group of friends at a local restaurant. At Gethsemani, however, meals were a communal affair. The monks gathered in the refectory at designated times for breakfast, lunch, and dinner. They sat at long wooden tables set with wooden utensils, earthenware mugs, water pitchers, enameled plates, bowls, and cloth napkins. The Trappist diet was strict: it included no meat, eggs, or cheese, so a typical meal consisted of soup, bread, vegetables, and an apple or a pear for dessert. And then there was the odd close of the meal, as biographer Monica Furlong described it: "After the Trappist had eaten, . . . the custom was to wash the knife, fork, and spoon in the drinking water, dry them on the napkin, empty the mug into the soup bowl, and dry it on the napkin, leaving everything in its original place on the table." Tom didn't particularly care for this ritual, but if he missed having waffles for breakfast, hamburgers for lunch, and pastries from the German bakery near his old apartment, he didn't complain.

Two other men were accepted to the novitiate at that same time so Tom had some company while he was learning. The three received regular instruction from the Father Master, whose job was to help them adjust to monastery life and to prepare them for Temporary and Solemn Profession. "[He was] a rather burly man with white hair and an extremely firm jaw," Tom recalled. "But as soon as he started to talk I found that Father Master was full of a most impressive simplicity and gentleness and kindness and we began to get along together very well from that hour."

Always an eager student, Tom listened well and learned quickly. He used what little free time he had to read religious books in the scriptorium (the monastery's library) and to write in his journal. On Feast Days, he at first used the interval of silence following the night office to write poetry. "After two or three hours of prayer your mind is saturated in peace and the richness of the liturgy," he wrote. "The dawn is breaking outside the cold windows. If it is warm, the birds are already beginning to sing. Whole blocks of imagery seem to crystallize out as it were naturally in the silence and the peace, and the lines [of poetry] almost write themselves." Both the Father Master and the Abbot Dom Frederic (the elected head of the monastery) were tolerant of Tom's need to write poetry. In fact, the Father Master encouraged Tom in his writing — even though he didn't have much time to do it.

What bothered Tom was what he saw as the lack of

genuine solitude at the monastery. The daily routine of the place took up a great deal of time — too much time, in Tom's view. "It seems to me," he wrote, "that our monasteries produce very few pure contemplatives [those who seek God mainly through prayer and reflection]. The life is too active. There is too much movement, too much to do. That is especially true of Gethsemani. It is a powerhouse. . . . In fact, there is an almost exaggerated reverence for work. . . . Doing things, suffering things, thinking things, making tangible and concrete sacrifices for the love of God — that is what contemplation seems to mean here. . . . [But] it is not without a touch of poetic license."

Nevertheless, Tom committed himself to this "active contemplation." He worked hard both in the fields and in the choir, where he was learning to perform church rituals. But his strenuous work — which had begun with good intentions — finally caught up with him: he ended up in the infirmary with influenza.

There he was given more balanced meals (meat, eggs, and butter were allowed in the patients' diets) and was encouraged to rest. But he was most pleased by what he thought would be an opportunity to regain the solitude he craved. "I remember entering the cell assigned to me with a sense of secret joy and triumph," he wrote, "[which] came from the thought: 'Now at last I will have some solitude and I will have plenty of time to pray.'" In *The Seven Storey Mountain,* he looks back on this as a time when he wanted to "indulge all the selfish appetites that I did not yet know how to recognize as selfish because they appeared so spiritual in their new disguise."

Was Merton being too hard on himself, expecting too much of himself? Monica Furlong thought so. Commenting on this infirmary visit, she said, "Tiredness, a need to be alone to rest and to recuperate from infection — simple and normal enough human states in themselves — are blown up into major 'sins.'" Nevertheless, Merton did realize during his recuperation that simply by wearing a monk's habit and adopting the Trappist lifestyle, he had not left himself behind in the secular world — his preferences, desires, and flaws remained with him. And he realized that the same was true of his companions.

Indeed, Tom's infatuation with the Trappists was gradually fading and was being replaced by a more realistic view. He concluded that monastery life, like secular life, was imperfect, and that monks were subject to the same human weaknesses — pride, ambition, laziness — as people in the outside world. "God had given me enough sense to realize at least obscurely," Tom wrote, "that . . . the first and most elementary test of one's call to the religious life . . . is the willingness to accept life in a community in which everybody is more or less imperfect." During the brief time he had been at Gethsemani, he had noticed that, among the novices, "there were one or two who exaggerated everything they did and tried to carry out every rule with scrupulousness that was a travesty of the real thing. They were the ones who seemed to be trying to make themselves saints by sheer effort and concentration — as if all the work depended on them, and not even God could help them. But then there were also the ones who did little or nothing to sanctify themselves, as if none of the work depended on them — as if God would come along one day and put a halo on their heads and it would all be over."

Tom's gradual awareness that even men who had lived for decades at Gethsemani were not saints but normal human beings came as a tremendous relief. If pride, self-discipline, and patience remained a challenge for *them,* then he could more easily accept his own faults. Perhaps, he thought, his need for solitude and his desire to write were acceptable flaws, ones that he could live with but that would require a certain amount of self-control. Still, he began to struggle with his desire to write. Was it a kind of self-indulgence? Was this yet another aspect of his former life that he needed to give up completely?

That summer brought the beginning of a different kind of struggle to Tom's life. His brother John Paul wrote to say that he had been training as a pilot, as a member of the Royal Canadian Air Force, and had recently gotten his orders to go overseas. He wanted to see Tom before he left. After John Paul arrived at the monastery, he began talking to Tom about getting baptized — but Tom quickly realized that his brother knew virtually nothing about the significance of the ritual. Thanks to the understanding of his superiors,

Tom was allowed to instruct John Paul himself for the next few days, and the baptism was performed at a local church. The next day John Paul left the monastery — and both brothers had the same sad presentiment, Tom recalled: "As the car [leaving the monastery] was turning around to start down the avenue John Paul turned around and waved, and it was only then that his expression showed some possibility that he might be realizing, as I did, that we would never see each other on earth again."

For the next several months Tom received letters from John Paul, one in which he mentioned that he was going to marry a girl he had met in England. Tom's reaction was ambivalent: "I was glad on account of the marriage, but there was something altogether pathetic about the precariousness of it."

By Lent of 1943, Tom had been a novice for a little over a year. He participated in the Lenten fast, and found that his senses were heightened tremendously: "Easter that year was as late as it possibly could be — the twenty-fifth of April — and there were enough flowers to fill the church with the intoxicating smell of the Kentucky spring — a wild and rich and heady smell of flowers, sweet and full. [And the] Gregorian chant that should, by rights, be monotonous . . . [sounded] rich and . . . spiritual and deep."

But Tom's sense of joy was darkened by the grim news that his brother's plane had crashed in the North Sea. John Paul had been badly hurt and had died a few

116

hours later. "Once again," Monica Furlong noted, "Merton had . . . to face the painful death of a member of his close family circle; his loneliness, and the insecurity of human love, had been reinforced once more. Now none of his immediate family remained."

Tom dealt with the loss as best he could. As any true artist would do, he turned to his writing in order to make sense of the tragedy and to put his feelings in perspective. The result was one of his finest poems: "For My Brother Reported Missing in Action, 1943." More than thirty years later, American folksinger Joan Baez read the poem and wrote a song based on its story. "[A friend] gave me a copy . . . and it set off one of those all-night confrontations with myself," she recalled. "I was very moved by the poem and wrote a song, from the poem mostly, finishing up about four o'clock in the morning. I knew his brother had died, and that night it was clear that if he could have given his life for his brother he would [have]. And so, in the song, he gives his life to his brother. . . . There was a generosity, a kindness, some sort of overflowing that I felt, and so I wrote 'The Bells of Gethsemani.'"

At Christmastime that year, Tom received an unexpected gift — Robert Lax, one of his best friends, made a surprise visit to the monastery. Tom was very happy to see him, and during their time together he gave Lax a collection of his poems. Despite Tom's ambivalent attitude toward his writing, and despite the fact that he had little time to devote to it, his poetry had continued to improve.

But even though he kept writing, he continued to feel torn between his desire to write and his commitment to the Trappist life. It was as if there were *two* Thomas Mertons: one who wanted to conform totally to the monastic life, and another who wished to retain the dream of becoming a writer. The writer had not disappeared when he entered the cloister and remained. The writer, who was "full of ideas," troubled the would-be monk, keeping "his imagination in a ferment." Tom sometimes commented on "the writer" as if he were another person: "He generates books in the silence that ought to be sweet with the infinitely productive darkness of contemplation." He even went so far as to say "One of us has got to die" in one of his journals. But this was a purely self-imposed pressure. Merton's superiors, in fact, were supportive of his writing and even encouraged it.

This ongoing tension, combined with long hours of manual labor, frequent fasting, a generally poor diet, and a lack of proper sleep, took its toll. Toward the end of his novitiate, Tom was close to physical collapse. He developed a cough, suffered shortness of breath, and endured intermittent fevers — and ended up back in the infirmary.

Fortunately, both the Abbot and the Father Master perceived that Tom's creative intellect needed a more regular outlet if he was to regain his health and reach his spiritual potential. Upon Tom's release from the infirmary, the Abbot reduced Tom's duties in the fields and farmyard, assigning him instead to translate French religious pamphlets and to research and write biographies of saints. In doing so, he relieved Tom of the temptation to "overembrace" the hardships of Cistercian life and provided him with an opportunity to use his talents in foreign languages, research, and writing.

The decision also reflected the Abbot's changing attitude toward individual behavior at Gethsemani. In the years before Tom arrived, a postulant's special talents and interests had been denied expression in favor of his conforming to the life of the community. Beginning in the early 1940s, however, this perspective began to change. By the time Tom became a novice, it was felt that "what was needed now . . . were those who had been trained as specialists before they joined, who would use their professional skills for the benefit of the Order."

Fortunately for Tom, Abbot Dom Frederic was himself a book lover. His father, in fact, "had been a bookbinder and publisher in the very town in Ohio where the Jenkinses [had once] lived and where Sam Jenkins had once owned and operated a bookstore." The Abbot therefore understood Tom's passion for books and writing and became a forceful ally in his literary career.

Tom accepted his new duties in the spirit of true obedience. Working mostly in the scriptorium on a typewriter he shared with another monk, Tom began writing religious histories and biographies for the

Abbot. Although the assigned writings were more scholarly than creative — not the kind Tom felt he was best suited for — he took them on without complaint. The assignments eased Tom's struggle with "the writer" inside him, though the conflict never disappeared completely.

On March 19, 1944, a little more than two years after coming to Gethsemani, Tom made his vows of Temporary Profession. At this point, he had learned most of the rituals of the liturgy, and he was accustomed to the traditions and duties of the Trappist order. Those who were already solemnly professed (that is, they had made a lifelong commitment to the Order) held a formal meeting and voted in his favor. Tom was then asked to sign over "whatever property he may have left" to the monastery and to write out "a long, formal profession in Latin promising stability, 'conversion of manners' (i.e., a conformity of his whole personality to the ideals of the religious life), and obedience to the Abbot." This accomplished, he received the black scapular, leather belt, and white cowl worn by those who were temporarily professed. The event was a milestone in Tom's spiritual quest.

In November of that year, he reached another milestone in his life as a writer: *Thirty Poems,* the manuscript he had earlier given to Robert Lax, was published. It is somewhat ironic that during the same year in which he took his temporary vows — including "conformity of his whole personality to the ideals of the religious life" — his first book was published. As it turned out, Lax had shown the poems to Mark Van Doren, who in turn had shown them to James Laughlin, the young publisher of New Directions Books in New York. Laughlin had already published books for such notable writers as Henry Miller, William Carlos Williams, and Ezra Pound. He liked Tom's poetry, and he was intrigued by the spiritual tone that infused his work. "There was a freshness there, a liveliness. . . . They were not like anything that any of the other New Directions poets were writing. There was an almost ingenuous character to them, which was appealing," Laughlin later commented. "What I liked was Merton's imagery and the way he could take a religious subject and carry it into real-life metaphors, so that I . . . was able to get a feeling, as I never had before, of what the Catholic faith was about."

Indeed, many of the poems included in Tom's first collection extolled the virtues of living in a religious community. "It is a book which works well to mirror the happiness this young monk felt," wrote Victor Kramer in his 1984 biography *Thomas Merton: Monk and Artist*. "[In it] Merton has begun to stop arguing with the world. . . . His concern is much more with celebration of having found a new way of life which allows a new perspective. . . . The comfort of nature and the pleasures of silence and prayer contrast with earlier times [in his life] when God was absent or denied."

Yet Tom himself was not particularly pleased when *Thirty Poems* was published — if what he recorded in *The Seven Storey Mountain* was the whole truth. He still had very ambivalent feelings about "the writer." But the Abbot was convinced that Tom should keep writing — and keep writing poems. Once again, Tom obeyed the Abbot's instruction.

In 1946, New Directions published Tom's second poetry collection: *A Man in the Divided Sea.* In addition to his original thirty poems, the book included about sixty new ones. Some of these, like "Ohio River — Louisville" and "Aubade: Harlem," were based on memories of places Tom had been and events he had experienced before he entered Gethsemani. Others, such as "After the Night Office: Gethsemani" and "Trappists, Working," concerned life in the monastery, and placed special emphasis on its beauty and simplicity.

In these two volumes of poetry, Thomas Merton the artist (though still wrestling with his talent) emerges at last, and the link with his father is powerfully clear. The gift of visual memory, an appreciation for the details and subtleties of landscape, and a need for solitude were characteristics he shared with his father. Like Owen Merton, Tom loved the simple things in life: the silence of the St. Antonin streets, the pure spirituality of the Privats, the long walks in the countryside around Olean. And he discovered, as most serious artists do, that a simplification of one's external life can lead to the expansion of one's inner life and creativity.

He realized that this was something his father had been trying to teach him, by example, all along. As a boy, Tom had accepted his father's restlessness, his rootlessness, his constant search for calm and quiet places to paint. Now, he understood how hard it must have been for his father to separate himself from the noisy, social, industrialized world long enough to develop his art. He appreciated, too, how difficult it was for his father, after his mother's death, to nurture both his family and his career. "[Tom] would never forget that he was by temperament an artist [and the] son of artists," wrote Victor Kramer. "[At Gethsemani], he gradually developed ways to combine his artistic talent with his intense desire to move closer to God."

Thirty Poems and *A Man in the Divided Sea* "attracted readers and notice"; the first printings of both books were sold out within three years of publication. Fan mail poured into Gethsemani from writers and poetry enthusiasts around the United States. But because the amount and nature of Tom's own correspondence were still limited (monks were now allowed to write two half-page letters four times a year), Tom could not respond to most of them. At his request, the Abbot granted him special permission to write more frequently to James Laughlin, under the condition that Tom's religious name — Father Louis — would not appear on anything that was published.

Tom agreed (though given how much the Abbot had encouraged — almost mandated — that Tom keep writing, Tom found this request for anonymity amusing). He wrote to Laughlin, asking him to send books and catalogs from New Directions. "What do you think would help me to write better, especially to keep the vocabulary from getting stale and me from getting into ruts, mannerisms, etc.?" he asked. What he felt but could not say directly in his letters (all mail was censored at Gethsemani) was that he also wanted to know what was going on in the world. Although the monastery provided quiet, it effectively cut him off from current events. When the atomic bombs were dropped on Hiroshima and Nagasaki in August of 1945, Tom was without newspapers, television, or radio. He learned of the event belatedly, and was therefore less aware of its psychological impact on the American public than he might otherwise have been.

Still, he understood the moral, ethical, and spiritual implications of nuclear war, and he was horrified that humankind seemed on the verge of self-destruction. In years to come, Tom would become an outspoken advocate of peace and human rights, even though his activism irritated his superiors. For the time being, however, he remained silent on these issues, making himself fit for consecration by practicing conformity, humility, obedience — and gratitude. "[Lord], I was created for Your peace and You will not despise my longing for the holiness of Your deep silence," he wrote in his journal. "I am content that these pages show me to be what I am — noisy, full of the racket of my imperfections and passions, and the wide open wounds left by my sins. Full of my own emptiness. Yet, ruined as my house is, You live there!"

CHAPTER 10

The Writing Monk of Gethsemani

In complying with the Abbot's wishes concerning his writing and translating "little books about Cistercian life and history," Tom produced a number of pamphlets and a few biographies. But he was not particularly pleased with the results. On the one hand, he wanted to obey his superiors; on the other hand, as biographer Monica Furlong pointed out, "he knew good writing from bad, . . . and if he must write, and his superiors thought he should, then it must be something at once more personal, more original, and generally of better quality than this raking over of past Cistercian glories. Merton was nothing if not a man of immense intellectual vitality and originality, and he began — surely with doubts — to try out a distinct Trappist voice of his own."

The result was that in March of 1946, Tom wrote a letter to James Laughlin telling him about a book he was working on called *The Seven Storey Mountain*. (Tom borrowed this title from a medieval miracle play that explored the seven stages of spirituality.) "Reverend Father just O.K.ed a new project — creative, more or less poetic prose, autobiographical in its essence."

Laughlin wrote back expressing enthusiasm for the project and asking to see the manuscript when it was finished. He knew that the country's interest in the religious life — such as Tom was leading — was at an all-time high. World War II had ended in August of 1945, but Americans were still stunned by its atrocities. They were hungry for books that addressed human-kind's spiritual nature, particularly those concerned with peace and forgiveness. The book that Tom was writing was just such a book, Laughlin believed. By retracing the path of his own spiritual quest, his attempt to find inner peace and to transcend his human ap-petites, Tom could bring hope to thousands.

Throughout the summer, Tom struggled to find time to work on the book. It was harvest season, and all day long the fields hummed with activity. Every man was needed, so Tom was allowed only two hours per day in the scriptorium. Seated across from Father Anthony, who was studying canon (church) law, he hammered out his rough drafts. It was a slow process at best. There was no one to help him organize notes, correct spelling, or offer editorial advice. He wrote a few different begin-nings, rewrote chapters, and made a carbon copy of each page he finished. In his next letter to Laughlin, Tom wrote, "About the prose — 7 Storey Mountain —

it did not turn out the way I thought it would at first. . . . It is straight biography, with a lot of comment and reflection, and is turning into the mountain that the title says. I cannot make it in less than 650 type-written pages. . . . Perhaps it would not be your dish, but I will certainly let you have the first look at it."

By the fall of 1946, Tom had nearly completed the manuscript. Despite his promise to Laughlin, however, he was reluctant to send it to New Directions. Because this publishing house specialized in shorter books of high literary quality (collections of poetry, essays, and short stories), Tom felt certain that no book as large as *The Seven Storey Mountain* had been produced there. Surely it would have a better chance of being accepted at a larger publishing house, one that published longer books such as novels and biographies.

As Tom pondered his dilemma, memories of his previous submissions returned. In the years before he entered Gethsemani, he had sent his first novel to Robert Giroux, a friend from Columbia who had become an editor at the prominent New York publishing house of Harcourt, Brace. Giroux had rejected the manuscript because "the story was without a resolution." But he did encourage Tom to continue writing and to submit any future work for consideration. Giroux knew from their days at Columbia that Tom was a good writer: "He [had] an eye for detail, for the apt image."

In October of 1946, Tom obtained the Abbot's permission to send the manuscript of *The Seven Storey Mountain* to Naomi Burton, a woman he had met at Columbia who was now a New York literary agent. He felt sure that she would help him find the right publisher for his manuscript. Tom included a letter, mentioning that Giroux might like to have a look at the book.

Burton received the manuscript promptly, but she was too busy to read it until early December. When she finally sat down to look it over, she liked what she saw. It wasn't a perfect book — too descriptive in places, with frequent repetitions and many undefined religious terms — but she was optimistic about its chances for acceptance. "I am interested in helping you find a form in which it would appeal to the largest number of readers," she wrote in a letter to Tom on December 9. "I don't mean that because of fame and money, but because you have something to say that might help others."

She then sent the book to Giroux, who became "quite excited about it." Like Laughlin, he was acutely aware of the public's needs and interests. "I felt the timing was right. This was the post war period, with a feeling of great disillusionment [in the United States]. Everything should have been changed by the awful war, but it became pretty clear . . . that nothing at all was changing, in fact it was going to start all over again [with the Cold War]."

On December 29, Dom Frederic gave Tom a telegram that said, "MANUSCRIPT ACCEPTED. HAPPY NEW YEAR." Tom was shocked to receive word so quickly, but delighted that Giroux had accepted it. He wrote to James Laughlin right away, explaining his reasons for submitting the book elsewhere and assuring him that New Directions would have the first option on all of his future works of poetry, essays, and short fiction. Laughlin was understandably disappointed, but he agreed to Tom's terms.

As Naomi Burton drew up the book contract and Robert Giroux began editing the manuscript, Tom's focus shifted to his impending consecration. In January, the professed monks voted in his favor, declaring March 19, the Feast of St. Louis, as the date on which he would take his final Solemn Vows.

The period between Tom's acceptance and the official ceremony was a time for him to assess his spiritual development and to think about his expectations for the future. It also gave him an opportunity to re-examine the reasons he had come to Gethsemani and to confess "his misgivings about his vocation." In a private meeting with the Abbot, Tom discussed these misgivings: "his desire for solitude, the temptation to join the Carthusians [a less severe, more socially inclined order], his feeling that he was an outsider at Gethsemani and always would be."

Dom Frederic, whom Tom came to regard as his second father, listened patiently. "He assured me," Tom wrote in his journal, ". . . that everything was quite all right and that this was where I belonged. In my bones I know he is quite right and that I am a fool. . . . As usual, I am making too much fuss about it." The Abbot's words helped Tom to put aside his doubts temporarily.

But Tom's feelings of alienation and his sense of being an outsider would return from time to time, and they were somewhat justified. Tom's unusual upbringing, though emotionally difficult, had made him more worldly, better educated, and more sensitive than many of his Gethsemani brothers. "He had needs and interests that very few people could have sustained for any length of time," observed John Eudes Bamberger, who joined the Gethsemani community in the early 1950s. "And he frequently experienced our shortcomings as personal frustrations. We were a pretty ordinary group of people, and he was extraordinary in many ways. He had strong feelings about certain things that we weren't sensitive to, and I think sometimes we disappointed him. . . . He had very high ideals and unusual gifts and I think special grace from God, and it took a lot to measure up to what he felt life should provide and express. And most of us just didn't have it, perhaps none of us did." But for all his differences with his brothers, he felt powerfully connected to them and to Gethsemani.

Of course, Tom was also set apart by his writing activities: he enjoyed the privilege of having time set aside to pursue them. But for the rest of his days in the monastery, he would struggle with conflicting feelings about his writing and how much time and energy he devoted to it. On the one hand, he needed the intellectual and emotional stimulation of writing. On the other hand, he wondered if he wouldn't be better off serving God in the traditional monastic way, writing less and praying more.

This conflict was closely tied to Tom's need for solitude, one of his confessed "misgivings" about Trappist life. Given how much time he devoted to required daily activities, communal worship services, and assigned and voluntary writings, Tom felt that he rarely had time to seek God, alone, in prayer. This troubled him so deeply that he considered giving up his own writing in favor of more solitary prayer. "I went to see Father Abbot yesterday," he wrote in his journal. "Once again I asked him if I could stop writing poetry and he said that he did not want me to stop altogether. As soon as I got in the room I brought up the subject of avoiding too much activity and remaining in solitude and being a contemplative and he said 'No' to everything. By this time it ought to be quite clear to me that Reverend Father is set on my writing books. So that is that."

The Abbot believed that writing was important to Tom's physical and emotional health, but he had other reasons for encouraging Tom to write. In the postwar years, the monastery was flooded with applicants and was quickly becoming overcrowded. Both private and church donations and profits from the Gethsemani farm had remained the same, however, so the monastery was deeply in debt. But Dom Frederic was a wise and practical man. He knew that Tom's writings could bring spiritual comfort to many in the secular world. And if those same writings became commercially successful, they would bring badly needed funds to Gethsemani.

Tom may never have discussed the issue directly with the Abbot, but he was smart enough to perceive the situation himself. In a letter to James Laughlin, he wrote, "The monastery has got itself twenty thousand dollars in debt, with building new monasteries. God will take care of us, but at the same time if you can put me in the way of making pennies by my writing . . . I mean where there is a choice of projects, I ought, under the circumstances to always be choosing the one that will mean more bread and butter."

About a month before taking his Solemn Vows, Tom made out a new will and gave his few remaining possessions — some clothes, a few books, and his old suitcase — to the poor. He asked to keep the wallet that his godfather, Tom Bennett, had given him for his eighteenth birthday, and the Abbot agreed. Ironically, just as Tom was permanently relinquishing his right to own property, objects, and money, his contract from Harcourt, Brace arrived in the monastery mail. The contract included a schedule of payments for the author's advance (a sum paid to the author before the book is published) and future royalties (a percentage of the book's profit from direct sales). "So the royalties of the dead author will go to the monastery," Tom wrote jokingly in his journal.

On March 19, 1947, Tom made his Solemn Vows during a special ceremony in the cloister. Afterward, he felt "a sense of deep union" with his brothers. "I am part of Gethsemani. I belong to the family," he wrote. Indeed, the six-year period between 1941 and 1947 marked the first time in his life that Tom had remained in one place, the first time he had lived with the same group of people for more than two years.

Throughout the late 1940s and early 1950s, Tom's Gethsemani "family" continued to grow. The monastery had been built to hold seventy monks, but now accommodated nearly two hundred. Despite the obvious physical and financial difficulties that overcrowding presented, Gethsemani held to its policy of "open admissions" for all postulants.

At the same time, however, plans were made to open a new Trappist community in Utah. In the weeks preceding its opening, the brothers held extended "conversations" (in sign language), speculating on who would be transferred to the new order. "This morning Dom Frederic announced the names of those who are to make the new foundation," Tom wrote in his journal on June 29, 1947. "My name was not on [the list]. . . . I began to fidget when he got to Father Valerian [the organist]. . . . I will miss Father Valerian. . . . Here I sit writing this, under the tree. He just walked by with a sort of homesick expression and made me a sign that he would pray hard for me to be sent out there, too. I made him a sign back not to pray *too* hard."

The founding of the Utah monastery relieved some

of the overcrowding, but it left fewer men available at Gethsemani to work the summer harvest. Tom felt torn between his desire to put in extra hours in the fields and his need to work on his writing projects. The church censors had insisted that he "tone down" passages in *The Seven Storey Mountain* that described his college parties and his relationships with women. He also had three other books in various stages of completion. *The Waters of Siloe* (published in 1949) was a complete history of the Trappist order. *Exile Ends in Glory* (published in 1948) was a biography of Mother Berchmans, a Trappistine nun. *Figures for an Apocalypse* (published by New Directions in 1948) was Tom's third poetry collection. The Abbot kept him busy with shorter projects, too. In addition, Tom was to write one brochure celebrating Gethsemani's one hundredth anniversary, another to serve as a guide for new postulants, as well as translate several more religious histories from their original French versions.

Not surprisingly, Tom felt increasingly burdened by his various responsibilities. He began to suffer from insomnia and showed signs of nervous exhaustion. He spoke to the Abbot again, voicing his concerns about being too busy to pray in the manner he felt God wanted him to pray. The Abbot assured Tom that his assigned writings had no urgent deadlines, and he suggested that Tom use his hours in the fields for contemplation as well as manual labor.

Fall brought cooler weather, and Tom progressed

slowly in his writing projects. He tried to use the beauty and harmony of nature to quiet his restless mind, as Dom Frederic had suggested. He also remained thankful for his gift of good humor, a characteristic that helped him keep his writing difficulties in perspective. "All the hills and woods are red and brown and copper, and the sky is clear with one or two very small clouds," he wrote in October. "A buzzard comes by and investigates me, but I am not dead yet."

Still, he continued to feel conflicted about his writing and his desire for prayer and solitude. By mid-March of the following year, he wrote in his journal, "At Communion it is Christ in the garden who prays for me. I don't feel like writing any more. . . . I am reading over the manuscript of *The Waters of Siloe* and cannot tell whether or not it is dull." And in mid-May he wrote poignantly, "O God, do not let me take away from You the time that belongs to You in contemplation." But less than a week later he wrote jubilantly of spring: "A tremendous bright sky. I let the warm sun shine on my back. . . . All the green of green things is clean and dark and fresh and the sun is so high . . . that the shadows of things are right under them."

About a month later he received page proofs of the index for *The Seven Storey Mountain,* which delighted him: "I was fascinated. The index is beautiful. It is like the gathering of all the people I have known at a banquet to celebrate the publication of the book."

Then, on July 7, Dom Frederic gave him the first

printed copy of the autobiography. According to biographer Michael Mott, "It seemed to Merton the moment was at least as significant to Dom Frederic as it was to him." But the pleasure that the Abbot took in this event could not conceal the fact that he was very ill. In fact, he died less than a month later — a loss that Tom felt deeply. At the beginning of August he wrote to Naomi Burton, "Our Father Abbot died suddenly and the monastery is somewhat upside down. . . . I suddenly realized how much I owed to this abbot who was in every sense a Father to us."

In a matter of weeks, Dom Frederic was replaced by a new Abbot, Dom James Fox, a former naval officer from Boston. The monastery's new leader "saw the faith in almost devastatingly simple terms. He had a favorite motto — 'All for Jesus, through Mary, with a smile.'"

This wasn't the only major change in Tom's life. The publication of his autobiography would also trigger a huge — and lasting — change.

Before the final bound edition of the book was printed, Giroux sent final copies of the manuscript to three well-known writers, asking for their comments. The response was genuinely enthusiastic. British novelist Evelyn Waugh wrote, "[This book] should take its place among the classic records of spiritual experience." British biographer and novelist Graham Greene hailed it as "an autobiography with a pattern and meaning valid for all of us." American writer and editor Clare Booth Luce "predicted that in one hundred years readers 'will turn to this book to find out what went on in the heart of men in this cruel century.'" Their comments, as well as orders by three Catholic book clubs, caused Harcourt, Brace to increase its initial printing order by several thousand copies. Confident that the book was going to sell out quickly, the publisher then ordered a second printing of the book before the first was even released.

As predicted, the book's first printing sold well. In October, the book sold about 6,000 copies. In November, sales increased to almost 13,000 copies, and by the end of December, stores across the nation had submitted orders for an additional 31,000 copies. "That last figure is significant," Robert Giroux later told a journalist. "In the book trade, it is usual for fewer orders to be filled [in December] than in any other month. . . . Christmas orders have nearly all been filled by the end of November. Yet between Christmas and New Year's [of 1948] the order clerks at Harcourt, Brace had one of their busiest periods in the entire year. New readers, all over the country, averaging *two thousand* every business day, wanted the book out of season, for its own sake, and they wanted it in extraordinary quantities."

Sales of *The Seven Storey Mountain* continued to climb during the next six months. In May of 1949, when Giroux visited Gethsemani to witness Tom's priestly ordination, he presented Tom with the 100,000th copy. Recent reviews of the published edition were very positive, Giroux proudly announced. A journalist for *The*

Catholic World had written, "[It] is a prolonged prayer as well as a great book." A reviewer for the *New York Herald Tribune* had commented, "[The story of] Merton's progress to the monastery is deeply moving. . . . There will be many [readers] who, however alien the experience may remain to them personally, will put the [book] down with wonder and respect."

It was glowing reviews like these, plus the enthusiastic response of thousands of individual readers, that made *The Seven Storey Mountain* a best-selling book. The original cloth edition sold more than 600,000 copies. The British version, *Elected Silence,* edited by Evelyn Waugh, also sold well when it appeared in Great Britain a year later.

The book's extraordinary success did not take Tom entirely by surprise; he had expected it to have a certain appeal among both spiritually inclined readers and general readers. But even he probably hadn't counted on its immense and lasting popularity. Royalties brought money to Gethsemani that was used to make overdue repairs and improvements. But as Tom's friend Ed Rice observed, fame had its darker side, too. "[The success of] *The Seven Storey Mountain* catapulted Merton into the eyes of the world, making a celebrity of a man who wanted to live in solitude."

Fan mail came pouring in. Tom struggled to keep up with it, but he found it impossible to answer each letter personally. The new Abbot, Dom James, made an exception in Tom's case concerning correspondence, and even assigned several postulants to help him. Despite this, Tom felt overwhelmed by the responsibility of having written a book that was obviously making a deep impact on people's lives. "The legend is stronger than I am," he later told a reporter. "I am doing my best to live it down."

CHAPTER 11

Seeds of Change

Thomas Merton was ordained in May of 1949. And although it was a profound event that he cherished, it did not mark an easy transition in his life. In fact, following his ordination, Tom endured a period of poor health that lasted about a year and a half.

It began that summer. Being a priest was satisfying yet challenging in numerous ways. For one thing, performing the Mass was an incredibly intricate task, and Tom sometimes had trouble getting through it. On one particularly hot day, he even fainted during Mass, and this increased the difficulty he had with it. Added to that were the ongoing stresses of too much work, too little sleep, and too little time for solitude and contemplation. And then came yet another task, another responsibility. In late 1949, he began teaching an introductory class in theology for the Scholastics (students for the priesthood), and began an orientation course for the novices. Because of the large number of postulants entering Gethsemani, the old system of instructing young monks — through one-on-one mentoring — was no longer feasible. Instead, a group of as many as forty postulants gathered in a separate classroom each week to receive instruction in the history and traditions of the Trappist lifestyle. Tom's teaching background and his affinity for young people made him a natural for the position — and yet it was one more demand on his time and energy.

After enduring months of being overburdened, Tom came down with the flu, which reached epidemic proportions at Gethsemani early in 1950. At one point, there were more brothers in the infirmary than out. "The infirmary is full," Tom wrote in his journal. "In the dormitory, there is a lot of noise, to which I contribute by my unsuccessful efforts to breathe. The terrible thing about sickness is that you tend to think you are sick. Your thoughts are narrowed down to your own little rag of a body."

The new Abbot's military training had left him largely unsympathetic to physical weakness. During the epidemic, he issued "a general request" that Brothers attend worship services if their temperature didn't exceed 101 degrees. Tom managed to drag himself to most of the services, but returned exhausted from the effort.

By late spring, most of the brothers at Gethsemani were fully recovered, but Tom's cough lingered. That summer he worked in the fields as usual, despite feeling weak and frequently short of breath. In September his condition worsened, and he was admitted to the hospital in Louisville. The doctors allowed him to return to Gethsemani in October but urged him to rest.

However, the monastery was such an active place and Tom was such an important part of it that prolonged rest was hardly possible. By November his cough had deepened, and he suffered from recurring sinus infections. He returned to Louisville, this time for antibiotic treatment and an operation on his nose. But things were more serious than that: chest and stomach X-rays revealed "abnormalities," another indication that Tom needed more rest. Interestingly, Tom offered vivid, often comic descriptions of his stay there. "This time I am on the first floor in the priests' corridor, which is a wild, amusing section of the world," he wrote in his journal. "There are other Trappists here. . . . Father Campion, a Passionist priest, is lying upstairs in an apparatus evidently designed by [surrealist artist] Salvador Dali."

In the past, Tom had often complained about "the commotion" of the secular world. But during his hospital stay, he observed everything around him with extreme interest and an almost childlike curiosity: "[The hospital] is full of people scrubbed and dressed in white. In this respect, it is like the movies. Uniforms. Everything is sterile. I think the most interesting thing about it all is that you are surrounded by people, mostly women, in white. . . . It is delightful." Even the nose operation he underwent was fascinating: "Dr. Rosen cut some . . . cartilage out of my nose. . . . It did not hurt. . . . Sister Helen Elizabeth stood by saying the rosary. A student nurse got sick. I sweated mightily. . . . Dr. Rosen sweated but less mightily. . . . [That part] was nothing like the movies."

After his operation, Tom returned to Gethsemani at the beginning of December, feeling rested. He plunged eagerly into his writing, finishing his next book, *The Ascent to Truth,* in just two months. In it he attempted to explain ways in which modern, secular people could develop consistent habits of prayer and contemplation. Although the book did not enjoy great success in the marketplace, it reveals much of what Tom had learned about religious belief and spirituality. "Devotion to God is impossible without an interior life," he said, and "meditation, prayer, and some degree of solitude are necessary [to attain it]."

But this was just one of a number of projects that were published about this time. Before succumbing to illness, Tom had managed to complete four of his five manuscripts-in-progress and had sent them to Naomi Burton for placement at various publishing houses. *Seeds of Contemplation,* a collection of essays on the contemplative life, and *The Tears of the Blind Lions,* his fourth collection of poems, were published by New Directions in 1949. That same year, Harcourt, Brace published *The Waters of Siloe,* a history of the Trappist order that Tom had been assigned to write under Abbot

Dom Frederic. In 1950, a biography of Trappist mystic Saint Lutgarde entitled *What Are These Wounds?* appeared.

Of this group, *Seeds of Contemplation* remains Tom's most popular and enduring work. In this book he expresses his ideas on spiritual development, addressing questions such as these: "What is the proper attitude toward human nature . . . toward material [goods]. . . . What is [our] proper relationship to God?" The book's essays challenge readers to discover that "each event, each creature [on Earth] is at once itself and a reminder of God and our vocation to union with him." In the preface, Tom acknowledged God's own grace in the writing of the text: "This is not the kind of book that . . . [can] be [entirely] controlled by any human author. If you can bring yourself, somehow, to read it in communion with the God in whose presence it is written, it will interest you and you will probably draw fruit from it."

Thirteen years later, *New Seeds of Contemplation* — a revised and expanded version of the book — was published. The central themes of the original — contemplation, compassion, simplicity, and charity — remained the same, proving themselves timeless in their relevance to readers of every generation.

And then there were the journals. Since entering Gethsemani, Tom had developed a habit of keeping two kinds of journals. The first he wrote in bound notebooks and kept for his own personal use. (The absence

145

of spoken conversation in Trappist life made personal writing one of the few forms of "conversation" available, and Tom took full advantage of it.) The second kind, which were intended for publication, he wrote in spiral notebooks. These constituted a sort of documentary of monastery life and, in particular, of his own victories and disappointments within that life.

In 1950, Tom sent part of one his "public journals" to Naomi Burton, asking if she thought it might be published. Burton's response was enthusiastic. "It is exciting to read something that knocks sparks out of the tired old brain," she wrote in her letter to Tom. "I am, irrationally, so proud of you and so grateful for you."

The Sign of Jonas, Tom's journal entries between December 1946 and July 1952, was published by Harcourt, Brace in 1953. Journals from other periods in his life, including the years before he entered Gethsemani, were later published as well. They include *The Secular Journal,* also called *The Cuban Journal* (1959), *Conjectures of a Guilty Bystander* (1966), *The Asian Journal* (1973), *Woods, Shore, Desert* (1982), *The Alaskan Journal* (1986), and *A Vow of Conversation* (1988).

Some saw Tom's desire to publish his journals as selfish and contradictory to his vow of silence. And despite how much Tom had published at this point — and how much more he would publish — he still remained uncomfortable in his role as a writer well-known to the public. Nevertheless, publication of his journals gave him a chance to share his thoughts, feelings, and spiritual growth with others. And though his desire for solitude remained powerful, his sharing of himself and his ideas was something he would do more of in the coming years.

His attitude toward his first published work — *The Seven Storey Mountain* — had already begun to change. His ordination had left him humbled: nothing less than God's extraordinary grace and forgiveness could allow a man with a past such as his own to become a priest. At the same time, he saw monastic life in less romantic terms than he had as a postulant — and it was this romanticized view of the religious life that readers of his autobiography had adopted. Tom also found it difficult to deal with the public's persistent identification of him with the book, even after he had moved beyond it. So in certain ways Tom came to regret the book's popularity. "I [have] left *The Seven Storey Mountain* behind [me]," he told a reporter at one point. "Certainly, it was a book I had to write, and it says a great deal of what I have to say [about God]; but if I had to write it over again, it would be handled in a very different way."

In May of 1951, Tom became Master of Scholastics, a new position created by Abbot Dom Fox. Technically this was the fourth highest position in the community, but in terms of real responsibility it was probably more important than that. Tom was not only "training the professed choir monks" but also "[serving] as their spiritual advisor under the abbot." He discovered that he enjoyed getting to know his students in this way. In a letter to James Laughlin, he wrote, "It is much more interesting than writing a book, besides being less fatiguing."

During the individual talks he had with students, he encouraged them to share their doubts, fears, spiritual victories, and special problems in adjusting to life at Gethsemani. During a particularly harsh winter, Tom observed, "Half of my spiritual children have colds and some of them are depressed . . . while two of them are trying to kill themselves with overwork. . . . I understand their anguish which, five years ago, was my own anguish. But I do not approve of their exhaustion." Tom knew from personal experience the dangers of being physically and emotionally overtaxed.

The emotional and social benefits of Tom's new position were hardly one-sided. Though he guarded his privacy fiercely and continued to have a strong need for solitude, he felt invigorated by his conversations with students. "The more I get to know them," he wrote in his journal, "the more reverence I have for their individuality. . . . The best of them, and the ones to whom I feel closest, are also the most solitary and at the same time the most charitable." Of the young ones, he said, "They come to me with intelligent questions, or sometimes with an even more intelligent absence of questions. They refresh me with their simplicity."

Tom's appointment as Master of Scholastics was just one of many changes that Dom James effected during his first years in office. His perspective on monastic life was less traditional than his predecessor's, and he saw a need for modernization. Beginning in 1950, he planned extensive renovation to the cloister, the dormitory, and the barns. This work was completed over several years, and largely funded by royalties from Tom's books. New heating and septic systems were installed, lighting was improved, and a temporary wing was added to the dormitory to house incoming postulants. Farm equipment was also modernized — horses and plows were replaced with modern tractors, and axes with gas-powered chain saws. Physical labor remained demanding, but output from the fields and orchards increased, thereby lessening the monastery's debt.

In the Trappist world, where change was rare and sweeping change almost unheard of, Dom James was clearly an exception. Tom missed his friend Dom Frederic — and he also missed things about "the old life" that seemed to have been buried with him. Though Tom realized that certain things needed to be changed or modernized, he also recognized the toll that was being taken on traditional Cistercian life at Gethsemani. Among other things, the noise made by the new farm machinery "broke the old contemplative peace." As biographer Michael Mott explained, "Some of the changes were both spiritually and physically damaging. It was not just that a pastoral idyll had been shattered. . . . Merton had a sure instinct that what was good for General Motors was likely to be very bad indeed for Our Lady of Gethsemani."

149

If Merton had certain problems with Dom James's relentless modernization, he was pleased with a relatively small yet significant change that Dom James made: he relaxed the rules concerning local confinement. He allowed professed monks to venture outside the stone-wall enclosure and to walk in the woods or near the road on the outskirts of the property. For Tom, whose opportunity for true solitude diminished each time a new postulant entered, this was a significant and welcome change.

This particular privilege was revoked by the French Abbot General, Dom Gabriel Sortais, when he visited Gethsemani in the early 1950s — a revocation that upset Tom deeply. Fortunately, Dom James was able to find a way for Tom to have some solitude while at the same time remaining obedient to Dom Gabriel. Because Gethsemani was surrounded by thickly wooded forests, small fires would often break out during the dry season. They were always brought quickly under control, but the threat remained that a larger fire could reach the monastery or damage the crops. And so, when the French abbot left, Dom James appointed Tom as Gethsemani's official fire warden.

Tom's new position as fire warden — as well as forester (Dom James put him in charge of restoring the woods, which had been stripped of their hardwoods in earlier logging practices) — meant that he could spend long hours alone in the woods. But Tom was searching for a more substantive kind of solitude than these combined jobs could offer, and this fueled his periodic urges to leave the Trappist order. Through his religious reading, he knew about the Carthusians and the Camaldolese (an Italian order). These more relaxed orders (and others like them) still attracted him. In fact, throughout the 1950s he would have "recurring crises" when he was very tempted to leave Gethsemani. But Dom James always responded with strong arguments for Tom's remaining at the monastery.

In the mid-1950s, Tom became particularly interested in joining the Camaldolese house at Frascati, and he wrote to another monk about the prospect. Dom James, aware of this situation, eventually wrote to Archbishop Montini of Milan (later Pope Paul VI), strongly discouraging Tom's proposal, claiming that it would deal a serious blow not only to his students but to many others as well:

> Concerning his relations with the outside world, both Catholic and non-Catholic, good Father Louis does not realize that he is a public figure of tremendous importance.
>
> In my travels, I hear comments on how much confidence priests and religious place in Father Louis and his writings. . . . There would be tremendous scandal to know that he is really quite restless and unsure of himself after having spent some fourteen years in one monastery.
>
> His influence as a writer would be destroyed in a marked degree.

Was the abbot being fair? According to Michael Mott, "The abbot always argued that it was essential for Merton's spiritual life, to his salvation, for him to remain at Gethsemani and in obedience to his vow of stability." Still, Mott pointed out, Dom James was very aware that Thomas Merton was both a spiritual and a financial asset to the monastery, and this certainly influenced the decisions he made.

Tom was very unhappy with this particular decision, but he remained obedient to his superior's wishes.

On the heels of this decision, Tom made a move of his own that was somewhat surprising. When the position of Master of Novices became open that year (1955), Tom asked that he be chosen for it. This new job — the third highest position at Gethsemani — required Tom to spend several hours each day in the novitiate (a separate wing of the cloister). He described the novitiate as "the quietest and most secluded corner" of the monastery, and he was also given a tiny room over the stairs — a room of his own at last. So there was a certain kind of peace and solitude that came to him in this way. But there were numerous demands on his time now, and besides reducing his time for solitude, they left him virtually no time for writing. In fact, in a letter to his friend Dom Jean Leclercq, a priest who belonged to the French Benedictine order, he wrote, "I shall cease to be a writer at least as long as I am in charge of the novices. The prospect does not trouble me. I care very little what I do now, so long as it is the will of God."

152

Tom did not actually stop writing completely, but his output necessarily decreased due to the long hours he devoted to counseling and instruction. Not surprisingly, Merton's style of teaching, counseling, and mentorship left a lifelong impression on his young charges. Many of the postulants who came to Gethsemani during this time had been drawn to the Trappist lifestyle through their reading of *The Seven Storey Mountain*. One of them remembers expecting "the great" Thomas Merton to be "serious and mystical-looking." Instead, he found him to be "boyish and lighthearted." Though ever obedient to God's will, Tom displayed a healthy disrespect for conformity and a disdain for unnecessary rules. "The first time I saw him he was bouncing down the cloister making all the signs we weren't supposed to make," this student recalled. "We were all going into the church and he was going in the opposite direction which I suppose was a part of the joke. He never wanted you to take him too seriously."

Although Tom enjoyed his teaching, his friends (with whom he corresponded and who visited him occasionally) saw something in him that his students probably didn't: he was deeply depressed about the Abbot's having rebuffed his interest in other orders. Tom's friends did their best to support him, and Tom began studying psychology on his own; Dom James even allowed him to leave the monastery to attend a workshop on psychiatry and pastoral care. But Tom's recovery was slow, maybe in part because he was trying very hard to achieve a difficult kind of balance in his life.

153

As he struggled to achieve this balance, Tom was once again juggling multiple responsibilities. Yet he still found time to spend outside the monastery, in the surrounding woods, which gave him the opportunity to experience and enjoy the simple pleasures of nature. In his journal entries of the 1950s and early 1960s, he mentions the beauty and simplicity of life in the out-of-doors more frequently and in greater detail than ever before. Early on in these writings there are suggestions that the artificial line that Western cultures drew between the human (civilized) world and the natural (uncivilized) world began to blur in Tom's mind. "The woods cultivate me with their silences," he wrote already in January 1952, "and all day long even in choir and at Mass, I seem to be in the forest." On February 2, Shrove Tuesday, he wrote, "I sit on a cedar log half chewed by some novice's blunt axe. . . . The hills are as pure as jade in the distance. God is in His transparent world."

Tom's reverence for nature grew, and as it did he discovered that feelings of profound peace and wholeness came to him as often in the woods as in the cloister. This inspired Tom to study Eastern religions, particularly Buddhism. With Dom James's permission, Tom requested books, through his editors and friends, on Oriental traditions, religions, mysticism, and meditation.

Through his reading, and through his correspondence with the Japanese scholar, writer, and philosopher D. T. Suzuki (which he began in the late 1950s), Tom discovered that Eastern and Western religious traditions had much in common: both emphasized compassion, peace, and tolerance, and both encouraged harmonious human communities. It was only the manner in which they expressed these common goals, as well as the path they followed to attain them, that differed. Tom learned, for example, that Oriental religions included a feminine aspect of God, while Western tradition emphasized God's masculine qualities. This insight caused him to gradually broaden his own concept of the Divine: "God is not only Father but a Mother," he wrote. "To ignore this distinction is to lose touch with the fullness of God." This was just one of the ideas that earlier Christian writers and scholars considered threatening or blasphemous. Tom, however, saw all human belief systems — with their various rituals, symbolism, and traditions — as complementary rather than conflicting.

In the years that followed, he continued to study both Eastern and Western religions. In his later writings — those published in the 1960s and afterwards — he attempted to explain their similarities and to suggest ways in which people from both cultures could share their richness. "Merton was really working, in his own language, in his own way of speaking and writing, helping people more to be than to have," observed Jean Jadot, a Belgian bishop who served at the Vatican in Rome. "I suppose that in the end his real role was to awaken people to the closeness in which we are living, the solidarity uniting all of us. Not only material solidarity, but spiritual solidarity too. . . . We are all the same children of the same father. Not such a new thought, I would say, but he, the prophet, the guru, let us see it once again — and clearly."

In March of 1958, while on an errand to the printer's (a rare trip beyond Gethsemani's grounds), Tom had an experience similar to the one he had undergone at age sixteen, when his father had "appeared" before him in the hotel room in Rome. As he stood on a busy street corner in Louisville, he perceived, on a profound level, his connection to all of humanity:

[I] suddenly realized that I loved all the people and that none of them were, or could be, totally alien to me. As if waking from a dream — the dream of my separateness, of my "special" vocation to be different. [But] my vocation does not really make me different. . . . I am still a member of the human race — and what more glorious destiny is there for man, since the Word was made flesh and became, too, a member of the Human Race!

Like all seemingly "sudden" revelations, this vision was a culmination of personal growth that Tom had been moving toward for several years. In his earlier days in the monastery, he had "turned his back" on society,

156

calling it "the wicked world" and writing (especially in *The Seven Storey Mountain*) in a highly romantic fashion about the religious life. Now, by contrast, he longed to embrace human life in all its wondrous forms. It is very likely that this was part of the balance he had been seeking.

That day in Louisville changed Thomas Merton for good, unleashing a flow of human love that he had previously held in check. He now vowed to turn back — emotionally and intellectually, if not physically — to the world he had once rejected, and to use his gifts to make it a better place. This was yet another incarnation of Thomas Merton: a man more keenly interested in solitude than ever, yet one who increasingly engaged the world and its challenges.

CHAPTER 12

A Different View

The late 1950s and early 1960s marked a period of enormous growth and change in America and in society as a whole. World War II had ended in a kind of false peace because the philosophical conflict between the Eastern bloc (communist nations such as Russia, Bulgaria, Czechoslovakia, Poland, and China) and the Western bloc (non-communist nations such as the United States, Canada, Great Britain, France, and West Germany) remained. Each side believed that its economic and political system was superior, and each accused the other of manipulating public opinion in order to further government interests.

This ongoing friction, known as the Cold War, exerted a powerful influence on the sense of safety and stability of democratic nations. Suspicion and distrust characterized international relationships during this period, resulting in a massive military buildup on both sides. After the horrors of Hiroshima, the threat of nuclear holocaust was as real as ever, but neither bloc trusted the other enough to give up its right to manufacture and, if necessary, to use nuclear weapons.

It was just about this time that Thomas Merton was deciding to take a more active role in helping to solve the problems of modern society. When he had first entered Gethsemani, he had turned away from the world with seemingly little regret. As he matured, however, his illusions about living a more perfect life inside a religious community disappeared, and he viewed the outside world with more compassion. With compassion came empathy and a growing desire for "involvement with [its] sin and suffering." In 1964, he published *Seeds of Destruction,* a book of essays on social problems such as racism, violence, and poverty. In 1965, he published a book entitled *Conjectures of a Guilty Bystander,* which he described in the preface as "a confrontation of twentieth century questions in the light of a monastic community." These were just a few of many indicators of Tom's increasing openness to and engagement with the world.

Tom had also reached a new level of acceptance about his writing: "If the monastic life is a life of hardship and sacrifice, I would say that for me most of the hardship has come in connection with writing. It is possible to doubt whether I have become a monk (a doubt I have to live with), but it is not possible to doubt that I am a writer, that I was born one and will probably die as one. . . . This seems to be my lot and my vocation."

Indeed, the immense success of *The Seven Storey Mountain* had made Tom one of the most sought-after writers of the twentieth century. His popularity had only increased over time, forcing Dom James to relax the usual rules regarding visitors and correspondence. There was a constant stream of guests flowing into Gethsemani, and Tom's desk never seemed to be clear of newly arrived mail. Although these intrusions from the outside world interfered with Tom's need for solitude, they also made him realize that he still needed social contact. They were also one of the means through which he educated himself on the nation's most urgent social dilemmas: poverty, crime, race relations, and war. He was horrified to learn that the United States had entered into a nuclear arms race with Russia, and that each country had stockpiled enough long-range missiles to wipe out the other in a matter of minutes. According to Mary Luke Tobin, the superior nun of a nearby convent who had gotten to know Tom and who was active in the peace movement of the 1960s, Tom recognized "the insanity in thinking that you could win a nuclear war, or even [survive one]."

To further educate himself about the world outside, Tom began to read voraciously — "poetry and politics, psychology and sociology, anthropology and environmental studies, philosophy and religion," according to biographer Monica Furlong. "His religious reading was no longer that of the 'good Catholic' — he was interested in Protestant writing and Jewish writing,

Buddhist writing and Hindu writing — what mattered to him was that the writers he read should have something important to say about the contemporary world and its dilemmas."

In the late 1950s and early 1960s, Tom wrote dozens of magazine articles concerning the most pressing and controversial social issues of the day. "It is my intention," he wrote, "to make my entire life a rejection — a protest against the crimes and injustices of war and political tyranny." As with all of his past writings, these articles were subject to censorship by the Church before passing into the hands of editors. At first, many of them were approved for publication in magazines such as *Commonweal, The Catholic Worker, Peace News,* and *The Saturday Review.* Eventually, however, Merton's views created widespread controversy among conservative Catholics who felt that he should restrict his writing to religious themes. "The Catholic community in the United States was, I would say, somewhat disappointed that the great hero, Thomas Merton, was talking about these social issues. They wanted him to talk about prayer and contemplation only, and only in their sense of it," said Mary Luke Tobin.

Tobin and Merton corresponded frequently. In their letters, they discussed a wide range of human rights issues, especially race and peace. Tobin recalled that Tom was "extremely interested" in the civil rights movement of the late 1950s and early 1960s. When several innocent black children were killed in race riots

161

in Birmingham, Alabama, Tom was appalled. "It seemed such an outrage to him," Tobin said; "you could see it in his eyes when he talked about racial injustice. . . . He suffered keenly because he identified so closely with those oppressed people. . . . He hurt as they were hurting."

As Tom's opinion of the outside world and the problems facing it evolved, he became increasingly frustrated and impatient with the restrictions of monastery life. "I think that we suffer (not least I myself) from the disease of absolutes," he wrote. "Every answer has to be the right answer and, not only that, the final one. All problems have to be solved as of now. All uncertainties are intolerable. But what is life but uncertainties and a few plausible possibilities? . . . Perhaps our problem here is that we prefer the security that can be gained by screwing everything down tight and keeping it that way, to the risk of letting people really discover themselves."

Previously, Tom had been obedient to a fault, believing that the Abbot's wishes — and the wishes of other superiors in the Church — represented God's will. Now, however, he realized that this was not necessarily so. The Church fathers had a right to their own ideas and opinions concerning problems that plagued modern society, just as he had a right to his.

But what is more — and it is here that he ran into trouble with censorship — Tom felt he had a right to express his thoughts on controversial issues while remaining a part of the Trappist community. His great popularity as a writer worked both for and against him. Because he was regarded as one of the foremost Catholic thinkers and philosophers of the twentieth century, nearly everything he published was promptly and widely read. Ironically, his very success led to increasing censorship by the Catholic Church. Both Dom James and the Abbot General believed that when people read an article or essay by Thomas Merton, a professed Trappist priest, they assumed he was speaking on behalf of the Church. Because so many of Tom's opinions and ideas differed from the official Catholic view, this created a delicate situation for everyone involved. For instance, many Catholics believed that war, while not desirable, was sometimes an appropriate response to unjust aggression. Tom, on the other hand, believed that "just wars" were irresponsible, a lazy way to resolve conflicts without doing the real work of negotiation, sacrifice, and compromise. In one of his letters that circulated privately (they were later published as *The Cold War Letters*), he challenged the official Catholic view on both war and birth control: "It seems a little strange," he wrote, "that we are so wildly exercised . . . about the prevention of conception (which is hardly murder) and yet accept without a qualm the murderous extermination [through war] of millions of helpless and innocent adults."

Public reaction was particularly strong following the publication of several articles on peace in *The Catholic Worker.* Dorothy Day, the magazine's editor, was a leader in the Catholic peace movement of the 1960s. Considered a radical by some, she often found herself at odds with authority, both inside and outside the Church. Not surprisingly, Tom and Dorothy had much in common, and the two frequently exchanged letters. Members of the Catholic Worker group, who allied themselves with Day, visited Gethsemani in the early 1960s. Conservatives labeled the group "communists" and considered the magazine to be anti-American. "There was anger [on Tom's part]," said James Forest, a poet who also corresponded with Tom during the 1960s. "He wrote me that the abbot general in Rome had heard from somebody in the FBI that [he] was being used by the communists. So, finally, he was silenced. He had just finished a book, *Peace in the Post-Christian Era*, and [the church censors] said 'Sorry, that can't be published.'" In fact, the Church forbade Tom to do any further writing about peace and war. "It was a time of intense suffering for him," Mary Luke Tobin recalled.

Not surprisingly, this intense period took its toll on Tom. He suffered from a number of health problems — colitis, bursitis, neck pain, and sinus trouble — which are frequently associated with emotional stress.

The controversy surrounding his writing and his friendships with "radical communists" that produced such physical and emotional duress left Tom discouraged but not defeated. Despite ongoing criticism from Church censors and an increasing reluctance on the part of Dom James to extend him special privileges, Tom was convinced that neither world peace nor racial tolerance would be achieved unless individuals learned to question political motives and bureaucratic authority. "With the race troubles in the South, one can see the beginnings . . . of a Nazi mentality in the United States," he wrote. "There is a powerful and influential alliance of business and military men who consider everyone who disagrees with them a Communist, a traitor, and a spy. The atmosphere is not unlike what I remember from the Germany of 1932."

Despite the furious controversy that surrounded him during this time, Tom was still Master of Novices, and he remained devoted to his students. They called him "Uncle Louie," a nickname he liked because it implied feelings of trust and warmth. In general, the novices of the 1960s were better educated and less trusting of authority than those who had entered Gethsemani in previous decades. Many, like Tom, were interested in the world's problems and regarded Tom as a role model for social activism. Ernesto Cardenal, a novice from Nicaragua who later returned there to establish his own religious community, learned a great deal from Tom — but not in the way he anticipated:

> I felt it was an incredible privilege to be instructed by this great master of mysticism who for so many years had been my master through his books. But when I

165

would meet him for spiritual guidance, he would ask me about Nicaragua, Somoza, the poets of Nicaragua, the Nicaraguan countryside, poets from other parts of Latin America, other dictators. He would tell me about his poet friends, . . . about his life in the outside world. . . . And at the end of the session he'd ask me if I had any spiritual problems, and generally I didn't have any so I'd say [so]. And if I did have any, he would resolve them in two or three sentences.

After I left, I'd have the impression that I'd wasted precious time that should have been devoted to spiritual guidance. Gradually, I began to understand that he was giving me spiritual guidance. Because at first I thought I'd have to renounce everything when I entered the Trappist order. . . . And Merton made me see that I didn't have to renounce anything.

He saw no conflict [between] the contemplative life and the life of action.

Although he derived great satisfaction from his role as Novice Master, Tom's desire for true solitude and release from the constant activity of the monastery remained strong. During recent years he had made repeated requests to Dom James to allow him to leave Gethsemani for an extended retreat. But Dom James, wary of granting Tom too much freedom, denied his requests. He was afraid that if he allowed Tom to travel freely outside the monastery, he might be tempted to leave Gethsemani permanently. (And, indeed, there were times that Tom seriously considered that very thing.)

Fortunately, Tom was able to "get away" to the little place he thought of as the hermitage. In 1960 the Abbey had erected a separate building within half a mile of the main cloister for the purpose of holding meetings and discussions with local clergy. This was part of an outreach program designed to strengthen understanding between the priests at Gethsemani and the ministers of non-Catholic churches nearby. Dom James gave Tom permission to use the building, when it was unoccupied, as a quiet place for reading, writing, and prayer. "A very fine little hermitage has been built in a nice site," he wrote. "I find that if I can have at least *some* real solitude and silence it makes a tremendous difference."

At first Tom used the hermitage occasionally, but gradually he began to spend more and more time there. Dom James, having given Tom permission to use the building, could do little to change this, and Tom remained insistent about his need for a retreat of this kind. His insistence produced results: after a while, during the weeks when no conferences were scheduled, Dom James allowed Tom to eat and work there, so long as he returned to the monastery for church services and sleep and fulfilled his duties as Novice Master. "I have had six full days up there, with more to come," Tom wrote to his French friend Dom Jean Leclercq in 1963. "What I have had so far is a great godsend. It has certainly settled any doubts I may have had about the need for real solitude in my own life." Eventually Tom was allowed to sleep there too, and he found that he slept well, away from the "communal noises" of the monastery.

The hermitage was very small — the size of an average family living room — with a tin roof and a wood-frame porch. The inside was sparsely furnished with a table, a desk, a single bed, and a few wooden chairs. A stone fireplace provided warmth, and there was a small kerosene stove for cooking. Because there was no indoor plumbing, Tom bottled fresh water from a nearby spring or carried it up from the monastery, and he used an unheated outhouse year-round. (Eventually the hermitage was "modernized" somewhat with electricity and running water.) In *A Vow of Conversation,* his published journals from January of 1964 to September of 1965, he described the small challenges and immense pleasures of being alone and close to nature. The entries he made during the winter of 1964 indicate his deep sense of wonder and gratitude:

November 2

A titmouse was swinging and playing in the dry weeds by the monastery woodshed. A beautiful, small, trim being. A quail was whistling in the field. . . . What a pure and lovely sound. . . . A tiny shrew was clinging to the inside of the . . . screen doors, trapped in the house! I took her up and she ran a little onto my sleeve and then stayed fixed, trembling. I put her down in the grass outside and she ran away free.

November 4

Lots of pretty little myrtle warblers playing and diving for insects in the low pine branches over my head. So close, I could almost touch them. I was awed at their loveliness. . . . [I had] a sense of total kinship with them as if they and I were all of the same nature.

November 24, Feast of St. John of the Cross

In the night, a rumpled thin skin of cloud covered the skies, not totally darkening the moon. It has become thicker as the morning wears on. There is a feeling of snow in the air. Streaks of pale lurid light over the dark hills in the south.

December 16

After . . . I washed the dishes . . . I looked up and saw a jet like a small rapid jewel, traveling north between the moon and the evening star, the moon being nearly full. Then I went for a little walk, and looked out over the valley. Incredibly beautiful and peaceful. Blue hills, blue sky, woods, empty fields, lights going on in the abbey. . . .

December 20, Fourth Sunday of Advent

Yesterday morning, as I came down to the monastery in the bright frozen moonlight with the hard diamonded leaves crackling under my feet, a deer sprang up in the deep bushes of the hollow. . . .

January 31

I can imagine no greater cause for gratitude on my fiftieth birthday than that, on it, I woke up in a hermitage. Fierce cold all night, certainly down to zero, but I have no outdoor thermometer. Inside the house, it almost froze. . . . The cold woke me up at one point, but I adjusted the blankets and went back to sleep.

Now Tom was finally getting a substantive taste of solitude — and with that came a clearer grasp of the fact that solitude, like life lived in community, was a mixed blessing, and in many ways a great challenge. As Monica Furlong commented, "He might yearn for solitude but he also knew that there were dangers attached to it, that it threw a man back on his own resources in a way that aroused anxiety, depression, and many other emotions. Even while he still worked in the novitiate, he observed that loneliness made it easy for a man to fall apart. . . . [He realized that] in the hermitage he would have to pray or go to seed, and the prayer would have to be a very genuine kind of prayer. But Tom was committed to this new struggle, and found himself capable, both emotionally and spiritually, of undertaking it.

In August of 1965, when he retired as Master of Novices, Tom was permitted to move into the hermitage permanently. Once again, he had shattered precedent by becoming the first American Trappist monk allowed to live alone. (Some monks in Europe had already been allowed to do so.)

Living in the woods, near ponds and streams and surrounded by birds and animals, gave Tom a new appreciation for the wonders of the nonhuman world. In nature's patterns and laws he found an inherent goodness, wholeness, and simplicity that seemed far removed from modern technological society with its waste and destruction. Before, Tom had appreciated landscape as a backdrop for human culture, but he had not really considered his own place in the ecological system. After he moved to the hermitage, however, he saw how God's goodness and truth appeared to emanate from everything in nature: "The happiness [here] . . . is so pure because it is simply not one's own making but sheer mercy and gift," he wrote in his journal.

Except for some writers, poets, and naturalists (such as Henry David Thoreau, Rachel Carson, and Ralph Waldo Emerson), relatively few people in Western society had linked the virtues of nature with human spirituality. Fewer still believed that the nonhuman world had any real value except to provide raw materials — wood, coal, hydro-electric power, food crops — for human use and consumption.

In Eastern religious traditions, however, nature had always played an important role. In Buddhism, for example, there exists a close kinship between all forms of life — animals, plants, and humans — and a profound reverence for beautiful places created by the forces of weather and geography. In this context, nature becomes a nurturing, feminine force from which people derive practical as well as aesthetic and spiritual gifts.

By 1965, Tom had already been studying Eastern philosophy and religious traditions for more than ten years. He saw that there were distinct differences between his own Christian tradition and religions such as Buddhism, Hinduism, and Taoism. Yet, despite these differences, he discovered "striking similarities" that he explored further in his writings. By this time, too, Tom had become determined to be heard on the peace issue, whether or not his superiors approved of his speaking out. Between 1965 and 1969, he published several books on Eastern religious philosophy in which he was adamant about the importance of peace, including *Gandhi on Non-Violence, The Way of Chuang Tzu, Mystics and Zen Masters,* and *Zen and the Birds of Appetite.* He wrote them in a style that is decidedly more open and fresh than that of his previous work. The brevity and simplicity of Oriental poetry and prayers no doubt influenced this change, which was not well-received by many American readers. "Many people refused to accept the work of the 'new Merton,'" said Daniel Berrigan, a Jesuit poet and social activist who was Tom's close friend. "They preferred rather a Merton in their own image . . . who [was] safe, and cornered, . . . and manageable." Some of Tom's contemporaries, however, welcomed "the new Merton": "It was the later writings on war and peace . . . and above all on Buddhism, that showed Merton at his best and most creative," wrote Tom's longtime friend Ed Rice. Writer J. M. Cameron agreed, observing in the *New York Review of Books* that "it is most likely these later writings that will stand out as Merton's most important work."

Besides his own reading, Tom's correspondence with Japanese philosopher D. T. Suzuki was his main source of information on Eastern spirituality. What was most surprising about this situation was that, for some mysterious reason, Dom James actually allowed Tom to visit Suzuki in 1964. Much to Tom's astonishment, Dom James gave Tom permission to travel to New York City, where the aging scholar was making a brief visit. There, Tom had "two good long talks" with Suzuki, whom he described as "ninety-four, bent, thin, deaf, but lively and very responsive." Tom found his secretary, Miss Okamura, "charming" and "extremely friendly." The three of them discussed Tom's books, the foundations of Zen Buddhism, and the common ground of Eastern and Western philosophies. "For once in a long time I felt as if I had spent a few moments with my family," Tom wrote in his journal.

173

Later that same year, Tom received an invitation from some Asian monks to visit a Zen monastery in Japan. This time, both Dom James and the Abbot General refused to let him go. "They say that this 'cannot possibly be the will of God for our order,'" Tom wrote somewhat angrily in his journal. "It has 'nothing to do with the contemplative life.' They have no capacity to understand the meaning of it." Nonetheless, he remained hopeful that someday, "in spite of everything," he might travel to the East.

CHAPTER 13

Final Journey

In November of 1967, Tom received a letter from his friend Dom Jean Leclercq, inviting him to a conference of monastic leaders to be held the following December in Bangkok, Thailand. The purpose of the meeting was to further communication and understanding between religious men and women from both Christian and non-Christian traditions. Tom was tremendously excited about it, but he was inclined to think that he wouldn't be able to go. Even though Dom James had announced his resignation, and Tom was quite sure that Dom James's successor would be more flexible on matters like travel, he still felt that such a journey probably would be out of the question.

But Dom James was replaced by Father Flavian Burns, a former student of Merton's who was more "broadminded" and "less afraid of external contacts." When Tom mentioned the Bangkok meeting in January of 1968, Dom Flavian was "open" to letting Tom go and promised to clear the request with his superiors. What's more, he suggested that Tom should first make a few shorter trips in the United States to find sites for future Trappist hermitages.

With this fortunate turn of events, Tom suddenly found himself with more freedom than he had had since coming to Gethsemani, and he planned to make the most of it.

In May, he traveled to Our Lady of the Redwoods, a Trappist convent in California. He gave a series of lectures there and explored the surrounding countryside, looking for a possible hermitage site. One place, "a deserted house at Bear Harbor" on the Pacific coast, he found particularly beautiful. He took some photographs and wrote Dom Flavian a glowing description.

He then hired a driver (he never learned to drive himself) to take him to San Francisco. There he spent the night at City Lights Bookstore, owned by the poet Lawrence Ferlinghetti, who admired Tom's work. From San Francisco, Tom flew to Albuquerque, New Mexico, to visit the tiny monastery of Christ in the Desert, located "thirteen miles by dirt road off the highway." He watched the ceremonies and dances of the local Apache tribe and took more pictures with his new 35-millimeter camera, a gift to him from a close friend.

He returned to Kentucky later that month, laden with several handmade Navajo rugs which the priests of the desert monastery had given him. He also brought back many rolls of undeveloped film, and a new journal (which was later published as *Woods, Shore, Desert*). The geography of the American West had made a powerful impression on him, and he realized he missed its wide-open spaces. During the trip he had felt homesick at times, but when he returned "he found himself longing to be either on the California coast or in the New Mexican desert."

The short trip west made Tom anxious to travel again, and he spent that busy summer planning his longer Asian journey. There were numerous details to attend to and arrangements to be made. He went to Louisville a number of times to obtain a passport (he had become an American citizen there in 1951), traveler's checks, and several dozen books on Asia. He read all of the books — some more than once — determined to arrive in Bangkok knowing as much as possible about Asian history, language, customs, and geography.

As plans for the trip became more firm, Tom found himself with a full itinerary. First, he would fly to Alaska to look for another hermitage site and to deliver a speech at a convent near Anchorage. Then he would travel to California to revisit Lawrence Ferlinghetti, who had recently published some of Tom's work. From California he would fly to Honolulu, Hawaii, then on to Bangkok via Tokyo and Hong Kong. He would tour India and Tibet before returning to Thailand for the monastic conference. If he was not too exhausted afterward, he would visit monasteries in Japan and Indonesia.

Tom reflected on the significance of his trip shortly before he left the monastery:

> I go with a completely open mind. I hope without special illusions. My hope is simply to enjoy the long journey, profit by it, learn, change, and perhaps find something or someone who will help me advance in my own spiritual quest.
>
> I remain a monk of Gethsemani. Whether or not I will end my days here, I don't know — and perhaps it is not so important. The great thing is to respond perfectly to God's will in this providential opportunity, whatever it may bring.

On September 11, 1968, he set off on the first leg of his Asian journey. He stopped briefly at convents in New Mexico and Chicago to give lectures on modern spirituality. He then flew to Alaska, where he stayed alone at "a pleasant house in the birches" near the town of Eagle River. He lectured at the local convent and talked to many of the contemplative nuns about their "anxieties and troubles." He spent much of the rest of his time there looking for a new hermitage site. He enlisted the services of a bush pilot to fly him over a remote Indian village where there was some land available. In his letter to Dom Flavian, Tom wrote, "Alaska is certainly the ideal place for solitude and the hermit life. . . . I am not in a position to decide anything yet, [but] I believe . . . that it would be very easy (in spite of obvious problems, weather, bears, and all that) to settle here."

From Alaska, Tom flew to California on October 2. After several days of moving from city to city, meeting a variety of people and giving a few lectures at Our Lady of the Redwoods, he went to San Francisco and spent several nights in a tiny apartment above the City Lights Bookstore. With Lawrence Ferlinghetti, the owner of the bookstore and the editor of City Lights Books, he explored the city and enjoyed the many sights. "I remember he was quite interested in any beautiful woman who walked by. A natural Trappist interest — why not?" joked Ferlinghetti. Another California friend, W. H. Ferry, recalled, "He was like a child on his first trip to Disneyland. He was at last on the last leg of the great adventure. He was full, full of a sort of quiet joy. He smiled a great deal, laughed a great deal."

Finally, on Tuesday, October 15, he was off to Asia. During the long flights from California to Hawaii and from Hawaii to Japan, he read the poetry books he had purchased in San Francisco and began making notes in a new journal (later published as *The Asian Journal*). After the flight from Tokyo to Hong Kong, he was getting restless and hopped out on the runway to walk around the plane and look at the night lights. This got him into trouble with the pilot, who promptly announced that "Passengers were under no circumstances to do this!"

Late in the evening of October 16 (having lost a day when he crossed the International Date Line in the mid-Pacific), Tom landed in Bangkok and was driven to a local hotel. At long last, he was in the Orient. "I have a great sense of destiny," he wrote, "of being . . . on my true way after years of waiting and wondering and fooling around."

His first excursion was to a Buddhist temple, where he met another writing monk. The two discussed their respective religions, comparing the paths by which Christians attempted to find inner peace and the Buddhists "mukti." Despite their traditional differences, they agreed that mental discipline was the key to spiritual freedom: "The mind is the cause of man's bondage and also of his liberation," Tom wrote in his journal, quoting the Indian philosopher and theologian Sankara.

Tom spent the next two days in Thailand studying Buddhism and visiting other Buddhist temples. Then he flew to Calcutta, India, to participate in a short religious conference in nearby Darjeeling. Because of severe flooding caused by the monsoon, representatives of ten different religions met in South Calcutta instead. The conference theme was the relevance of religion in the modern world. Tom made a speech in which he supported religious tolerance and an openness to different points of view. "Each person should be faithful to his own search," he declared. He spoke in favor of growth and change but warned against casting all of the old religious traditions aside: "In the West there is now going on a great upheaval in monasticism, and much that is of undying value is being thrown away irresponsibly, foolishly, in favor of things that are superficial and showy. . . . I do not know how the situation is in the East, but I will say as a brother from the West to Eastern monks, be a little careful. The time is coming when you may face the same situation."

In Calcutta — which Tom referred to as "the big, beat-up, teeming, incredible city" — he was overwhelmed by the poverty he saw. No matter where he turned, he was besieged by beggars. "When you give money to one, a dozen [more] half kill themselves running after your cab," he wrote in his journal. Despite the presence of poverty and despair, Tom found many things to admire about the Indian people and their culture. In his journal, he described the intoxicating smell of their spicy foods, the dark-skinned women dressed in brightly colored veils, the haunting rhythms of the Indian sitar (a stringed instrument), and the many exotic animals for sale in the marketplace. At night, he took part in the Buddhist festival of Divali (Feast of Lights), setting off a few loud firecrackers for the occasion.

While in Calcutta, he received a telegram from the secretary of the Dalai Lama, the exiled religious leader of six million Tibetan Buddhists. Before leaving the United States, Tom had written to the Dalai Lama, asking permission to visit him before the Bangkok conference. The telegram confirmed that a meeting was arranged for early November at the Dalai Lama's residence at Dharamsala, Tibet.

Tom left Calcutta, flew to New Delhi, and then, at the end of October, traveled by train and jeep into the mountainous regions of northern India. On the way, he took every opportunity to observe and study India's culture and religious traditions. Through his contact with monks and Buddhist leaders, he hoped to uncover the particular aspects of Eastern philosophy that were shared by Christians in the West. Tom believed that these aspects, once identified, would form the basis for greater religious tolerance and a deeper understanding between leaders — both political and religious — in the two hemispheres. "The horizons of the world are no longer confined to Europe and America," Tom concluded. "We have to gain new perspectives."

He toured ashrams (religious communities where disciples live and worship together under the guidance of a spiritual master or "guru"), prayed in Buddhist and Hindu temples, and visited Tibetan hermits. He learned that even in the remote mountain regions, true solitude was difficult to attain: "There are few places [here] where one does not run into someone. Roads and paths and trails are full of people. To have real solitude one would have to get very high up and far back!" From a Buddhist priest, he learned more about the Eastern practice of meditation and how to use a mandala (a small diagram used in meditation, often representing the universe) to reach alternate states of consciousness.

On November 4, Tom had his long-awaited meeting with the Dalai Lama. "The Dalai Lama is most impressive as a person. He is strong and alert, bigger than I expected," Tom wrote in his journal. "A very solid, energetic, generous, and warm person — very capably trying to handle enormous problems." The two men discussed many subjects concerning human spirituality and speculated on the future of religions under various forms of government. They both realized that as technology brought people from all corners of the world closer together, the need for compassion and understanding — as opposed to war and competition — would greatly increase.

A deep bond grew out of this first meeting, and the Dalai Lama invited Tom to return for two additional meetings. "[When] I looked in his face," the Buddhist leader later recalled, "I could see a good human being. . . . You can tell people who have some deep experience. . . . I could see he took a deep interest in Eastern philosophy, mainly Buddhism, and meditation. And he had an excellent understanding. He was very open-minded. . . . Such a person, I think, was very useful in this period, when the West and East were just coming to know each other. . . . Different races, different ideologies, different religions are sometimes dividing, sometimes the source of conflict, of problems. But if you apply the different religions, different philosophies, in the right way, all are [the] same."

At the conclusion of the third meeting, the two men

parted reluctantly. (The Dalai Lama was forbidden by the Communist government to leave Dharamsala, and therefore would not be attending the Bangkok conference.) "At the end I felt we had become very good friends," Tom wrote, "and were somehow quite close to one another. I felt a great respect and fondness for him as a person and feel too that there was a real spiritual bond between us." Tom promised to send his new friend copies of current magazines such as *Time, Life,* and *Reader's Digest* and to correspond with him when he returned to Gethsemani.

Merton made a brief trip back to Delhi, then to Calcutta. After that, he traveled to Darjeeling and enjoyed a few days' rest as the guest of a European couple who owned a tea plantation near there. He was tired and had a bad cold, and as he rested he realized that he had mixed feelings about his journey thus far: "Too much movement. Too much 'looking for' something: an answer, a vision, 'something else.' . . . I am still not able fully to appreciate what this exposure to Asia has meant. There has been so much — and yet also so little." But this feeling was soon to change.

After recovering from his cold, he went back to Darjeeling and Calcutta briefly, and then, on Tuesday, November 26, traveled south to the eastern coast of India, to Madras, where he visited Mahabalipuram, famous for the Seven Pagodas, the shrines on its seashore. "The trip to Mahabalipuram was fine," he wrote in his journal. "Especially the South Indian landscape under monsoon clouds. Dark green foliage, bright green paddy, thousands of tall palms, sheets of bright water, blue mountains in the south with fine shapes. . . . Then the sea, and the little thatched huts of the fishing villages. In a way this was more charming than anything I had seen in India — more peaceful, more relaxed, better kept. Here one finally got some sense of what rural India might once have been." Tom photographed the Seven Pagodas, "a complex of shrines carved out of, or built into, a great ancient rock formation . . . smoothed and shaped by millions of years."

After just a few days in Madras, Tom flew to Ceylon (now Sri Lanka). There he visited the settlement of Kandy, known for its many cave-dwelling hermits and for the giant stone statues of Buddha at Polonnaruwa nearby. At Polonnaruwa, Tom had one of the most profound mystical experiences of his life, which he recorded in his *Asian Journal:* "Looking at these figures I was suddenly, almost forcibly, jerked clean out of the habitual, half-tied vision of things, and an inner clearness, clarity, as if exploding from the rocks themselves, became evident and obvious. . . . I don't know when in my life I have ever had such a sense of beauty and spiritual validity running together in one aesthetic illumination. Surely with Mahabalipuram and Polonnaruwa my Asian pilgrimage has come clear and purified itself. I mean, I know and have seen what I was obscurely looking for. I don't know what else remains but I have now seen and have pierced through the surface and have got beyond the shadow and the disguise."

A few days after this powerful experience, Tom journeyed to Thailand, arriving in Bangkok on December 6. He spent a few days at the Oriental Hotel, making arrangements to spend over a week in Indonesia after the upcoming conference. He also wrote a short letter to Patrick Hart, commenting that "with Christmas approaching I feel homesick for Gethsemani." According to his plans, he would be spending Christmas in a foreign monastery.

Tom set off for the conference center in Bangkok on December 8. He was assigned to a room on the first floor of one of the two-story bungalows owned by the Red Cross. Other monastic leaders — both nuns and priests — were arriving from the airport and settling into their rooms in the compound. That evening Tom attended a reception that made him a bit uncomfortable. He tried to make himself inconspicuous, but that wasn't really possible; as far as the other guests were concerned, he was "the most celebrated and the most popular person there."

The conference began the following day, with lectures in the morning, group sessions in the afternoon, and informal discussions in the evening. There were short breaks for prayers and meals, and a scheduled rest after lunch — but Tom had no time to rest that day. He also found himself in the public eye: several international reporters were present, along with teams from two foreign TV stations. By the end of the evening, Tom was glad to return to his room for some quiet and rest.

The next morning, December 10, the entire delegation gathered to hear Tom's speech, entitled "Marxism and Monastic Perspectives." (Marxism, named after the nineteenth-century German philosopher Karl Marx, was a social system that sought to erase the boundaries of class and race.) "[When] Merton came to the lectern, there was utter silence," recalled Abbot Rembert Weakland, one of the major organizers of the conference. "Here was the most famous monk in the world about to share with us his profound thoughts. He wore his monastic habit . . . his delivery was clear and good — not excessively emotional, more like a class lecture."

Many in the audience, however, were surprised by the content of Merton's speech. They had expected him to speak about monasticism in the context of religion and culture, and to leave politics out of it. But Tom believed that all of these social factors were related. The outbreak of the Vietnam War and the experience of his own Asian journey proved that political differences certainly did affect relations between countries and their religious communities. Abbot Weakland speculated on how Tom might have written the speech: "I have a suspicion that he started it after he was on his Asian journey, after he had visited some areas of the Orient and probably had seen the real conflict over there. It was not a monastic conflict. It was an ideological conflict between Marxists and capitalists, and therefore, he focused in on what monasticism would be about in that kind of world."

Tom appeared tired and overheated after the speech. No doubt he had felt uncomfortable in front of the television cameras, and he told a colleague he was looking forward to a cool shower and a nap. He excused himself early from lunch and returned to the bungalow.

Sometime before three P.M., a French priest whose room was above Tom's thought he heard "a cry and the sound of something falling." He immediately went downstairs to see if everything was all right. He knocked on Tom's door and called to him, but when he got no reply, he assumed Tom was asleep. Many people were returning from lunch at that time, and the compound was noisy. The priest concluded that he had "imagined" the sounds and went back upstairs.

About an hour later, the same priest returned to make sure Tom was all right and awake for the late afternoon sessions. Again, he knocked and called. This time he felt that something might be wrong, so he peered through the narrow slats in the door. What he saw was alarming: "Father Merton lying in an odd way, a standing fan . . . lying on top of him." The door was locked, so he ran for help. The three priests who came to his aid managed to unlock the door from the outside by reaching in through the open glass window at the top. They hurried over to Tom. One priest grasped the fan, but he received a strong electrical shock that "threw him sideways." Fortunately, another priest unplugged the fan's cord from the wall and was able to remove the fan safely.

Tom did not move. Together the priests gave him absolution (pronouncing forgiveness of sins), and one of them left to get a priest who could perform extreme unction (a ceremonial anointing of oil). Another priest sent for one of the nuns, who was a qualified physician.

The doctor arrived a few minutes later. She examined the body and, finding no pulse, pronounced Thomas Merton dead. Abbot Weakland arrived, followed shortly by the Bangkok police and the coroner. The police investigated the scene and questioned the priests who had found the body. By this time, word of the incident had spread, and curious bystanders were crowding around the entrance. With Abbot Weakland's help, the police closed off the area and continued their investigation.

Meanwhile, at Gethsemani, Dom Flavian received a phone call from the U.S. State Department, telling him that Father Merton had died unexpectedly in Bangkok. "I was shocked," the Abbot remembers. "I took some time out and made a visit to the chapel and said a few prayers and took a walk around the monastery and came back to my office. . . . Eventually I got through to the embassy in Bangkok and they confirmed it. . . . So then we called in Patrick Hart as we wanted to inform all of Father Louis's friends before they heard it in the public announcements. And it was Brother Patrick who was the first one to really break down; he just collapsed in the chair and wept when he heard it. It was a very painful period for all of us. He was a beloved man. He was our Father Louis, not so much the world's Thomas Merton."

The police investigation was completed in a few days. The official report was that Thomas Merton suffered a heart attack, which caused him to fall and collide with the fan. But a police investigator had reported that there was faulty wiring in the fan that could have caused electrocution and possibly prompted the heart attack.

It was an unusual ending to a highly unusual life and was not without at least one bizarre coincidence: the date of Merton's death — December 10 — was the same date he had entered Gethsemani twenty-seven years earlier. This, and the fact that Merton had made some enemies by tackling controversial issues, led to some speculation that his death was not accidental. Rumors of suicide and even murder circulated long after the official investigation was concluded. Nothing was found, however — in the police report, in Tom's letters or journals, or in testimony by dozens of people interviewed shortly after his death — to support these rumors. "It was quite a long while before anybody really accepted that this was just an accident," said Tom's friend W. H. Ferry. "I now do, but I didn't for some time. His death left a hole in the lives of many people — never to be filled."

On December 11, Thomas Merton's body was taken

to the U.S. army hospital in Bangkok. Because of his fame and the unusual circumstances surrounding his death, an enormous amount of paperwork and several official clearances were required before the body could be returned to the United States. Arrangements were finally made, however, and several days later the casket was loaded into the cargo bay of an American military plane bound for California. Ironically, the plane also carried the bodies of servicemen killed in Vietnam, victims of a war that Tom had protested since its beginning.

In California, the casket was transferred to a regular commercial jet and flown to Louisville, where Dom Flavian and a small group of Trappists awaited its arrival. The casket was then taken to New Haven (near Gethsemani), where the body was positively identified. Biographer Monica Furlong described Tom's final return to the monastery: "The remains of Father Louis arrived at Gethsemani early on the afternoon of December 17th. . . . He had, after all, returned home in time for Christmas."

Dom Flavian delivered the homily at the funeral Mass, which was held in the Abbey's church. "The world knew him from his books; we knew him from his spoken word . . . [and] we respected him as the spiritual master of our souls," he said. The afternoon was cold and damp. A mixture of snow, sleet, and freezing rain fell on the silent monks as they gathered in the cemetery at dusk. There, Father Louis's body was laid to rest among the Gethsemani brothers who had passed before him, his plot marked, like the rest, with a simple white cross. As a tribute to Tom's faith and his writing, one of the priests read from the last chapter of Tom's autobiography: "And I shall lead you into the high places of my joy and you shall die in Me and find all things in My mercy which has created you for this end."

Gethsemani had lost a brother, America had lost one of its most respected writers and thinkers, and many others around the world had lost a dear friend and spiritual mentor. Yet even today, the fruits of Tom's labors — his teaching, his writing, his relationships with people from all walks of life and from many different cultures — bear testimony to the depth of his Christian faith and to his love for humankind. "He's living in each of us now," says Maurice Flood, a monk who entered Gethsemani when Tom was Master of Novices, "and we are grateful for that. That's what gives us the courage and the strength, the bouyancy to go on, knowing that this man has gone before us."

My Sources for This Book

In researching this biography, I was led on an all-absorbing journey into the personal and spiritual life of Thomas Merton — a gifted poet (in verse and in prose), a modern prophet, and a radical priest. The task of condensing his active life and prolific writing career into a book of this size proved more challenging than I had originally anticipated. The more I learned about Merton's life, both before and after he entered Gethsemani, the more I realized that no single volume could possibly do him justice. Ideally, anyone wishing to fully understand Merton and his impact on literature, religious thought, and human spirituality should read, in addition to this biography, several of his own books and journals. In the "Suggestions for Further Reading," I've listed those that I believe are both comprehensive and accessible to young adults.

Several previously published biographies were helpful to me in researching this book. Monica Furlong's *Merton: A Biography* (Harper & Row, 1980), and Michael Mott's *The Seven Mountains of Thomas Merton* (Houghton Mifflin, 1984) gave me a thorough overview of his childhood, education, and family life, as well as some interesting insights into his years at the monastery. Merton's autobiography, *The Seven Storey Mountain* (Harcourt, Brace, 1948), gave me insight into his emotional struggles, especially during the periods preceding his religious conversion and his decision to enter Gethsemani. His triumphs and disappointments while living among the Trappists were most thoroughly revealed in his journals, including *The Sign of Jonas* (Harcourt, Brace, 1953), *Conjectures of a Guilty Bystander* (Doubleday, 1966), and *The Asian Journal* (New Directions, 1973). Paul Wilkes's wonderful video documentary entitled *Merton: A Film Biography,* and the book he edited to accompany it, *Merton: By Those Who Knew Him Best* (Harper & Row, 1984), gave me a visual and social context in which I could frame Tom Merton's personal and spiritual evolution. I am deeply grateful to all of these authors for helping me to bring this book to fruition.

Suggestions for Further Reading

Forest, James. *Thomas Merton: A Pictorial Biography.* Ramsey, N.J.: Paulist Press, 1981.

Written by Merton's friend and colleague in the peace movement of the 1960s, this book contains "the most extensive collection of Merton photographs ever assembled." There is frank discussion about Tom's early promiscuity, but the book gives an excellent overview of his life. Most suitable for ages 12 and up.

Hart, Brother Patrick, ed. *Thomas Merton, Monk: A Monastic Tribute.* Kalamazoo, Mich.: Cistercian Publications, 1983.

This book focuses on Merton's spiritual life, social activism, and contribution as a "bridge-builder" between religious leaders in the East and West. Each chapter is written by a monk or nun who knew Father Louis personally. The book is intended for adults, but written in a style accessible to younger readers.

Kent, Deborah. *Dorothy Day: Friend to the Forgotten.* Grand Rapids: Eerdmans Publishing Company, 1996.

Dorothy Day was a friend and frequent correspondent of Merton. This portrait of her (written for young adult readers) documents her conversion to Catholicism, her experiences as editor of the controversial paper *The Catholic Worker,* and her tireless efforts to increase public awareness of the plight of America's poor.

Merton, Thomas. *The Asian Journal of Thomas Merton.* Edited by Naomi Burton Stone, Brother Patrick Hart, and James Laughlin. New York: New Directions, 1973.

This is a collection of Merton's notes, observations, and "jottings" about his trip to the East. The style is loose and informal and reveals much about his beliefs concerning those aspects of human spirituality shared by Eastern and Western societies.

Merton, Thomas. *The Sign of Jonas.* New York: Harcourt, Brace, 1953.

This journal covers Merton's years at Gethsemani from 1947 to 1952. In the prologue, Merton explains some of the particular customs and habits of the Trappists, thereby providing a context for the subsequent diary entries. This is a pleasant book to read because of its variety — it contains religious meditations, observations of nature, accounts of daily life in the monastery, and numerous examples of Merton's warm, intelligent humor.

Merton, Thomas. *A Vow of Conversation: Journals, 1964-1965.* Edited by Naomi Burton Stone. New York: Farrar, Straus & Giroux, 1988.

This journal, edited by Merton's literary agent, covers a particularly turbulent period in his life. It was during this time that he began living at the hermitage, confronted ongoing health problems, considered leaving the monastery, and plunged into controversial social activism. Scattered throughout the entries are brief essays on solitude, nature, and Oriental mysticism.

Wilkes, Paul. *Merton: By Those Who Knew Him Best.* San Francisco: Harper & Row, 1984.

This is a unique and highly readable collection of interviews with men and women who knew Merton both personally and professionally. Included is an excellent bibliography of writings by and about Merton.

Wilkes, Paul, producer. *Merton: A Film Biography.* New York: First Run Features, 1984.

A video companion to the above book, this hour-long documentary re-creates Merton's life from birth to death. It includes footage of his childhood homes, the boarding schools and universities he attended, the Gethsemani monastery, and a number of his destinations in Asia. Interspersed throughout the narrative are interviews with friends, religious figures, and writing associates. This is a very thorough yet entertaining film.

Selected Bibliography

The Ascent to Truth. New York: Harcourt Brace Jovanovich, 1981.

The Asian Journal of Thomas Merton. Edited by Naomi Burton Stone, Patrick Hart, and James Laughlin. New York: New Directions, 1973.

A Catch of Anti-Letters. Thomas Merton and Robert Lax. Mission, Kans.: Sheed, Andrews & McMeel, 1978.

The Collected Poems of Thomas Merton. New York: New Directions, 1977.

Conjectures of a Guilty Bystander. Garden City, N.Y.: Doubleday, 1966.

Disputed Questions. New York: Farrar, Straus & Cudahy, 1960.

The Literary Essays of Thomas Merton. Edited by Patrick Hart. New York: New Directions, 1981.

The Monastic Journey. Edited by Patrick Hart. New York: Doubleday, 1978.

My Argument with the Gestapo: A Macaronic Journal. New York: New Directions, 1975.

New Seeds of Contemplation. Revised Edition. New York: New Directions, 1972.

No Man Is an Island. New York: Harcourt Brace Jovanovich, 1978.

The Nonviolent Alternative. New York: Farrar, Straus & Giroux, 1980.

Original Child Bomb. Greensboro, N.C.: Unicorn Press, 1982.

Seasons of Celebration. New York: Farrar, Straus & Giroux, 1977.

The Secular Journal. New York: Farrar, Straus & Cudahy, 1959.

Seeds of Destruction. New York: Farrar, Straus & Cudahy, 1964.

The Seven Storey Mountain. New York: Harcourt Brace Jovanovich, 1978.

The Sign of Jonas. New York: Harcourt Brace Jovanovich, 1979.

The Waters of Siloe. New York: Harcourt Brace Jovanovich, 1979.

The Way of Chuang Tzu. New York: New Directions, 1969.

The Wisdom of the Desert. New York: New Directions, 1970.

Woods, Shore, Desert: A Notebook, May 1968. Santa Fe: Museum of New Mexico Press, 1983.

Zen and the Birds of Appetite. New York: New Directions, 1968.

Acknowledgments

The author and publisher gratefully acknowledge permission to quote the following materials:

Excerpts from *Merton: A Biography* by Monica Furlong. Copyright © 1980 by Monica Furlong. Reprinted by permission of HarperCollins Publishers, Inc. English-language rights outside the U.S. and Canada granted by Sheil Land Associates.

Excerpts from *Merton: By Those Who Knew Him Best,* published by HarperCollinSanFrancisco. Copyright © 1984 by Paul Wilkes. Used with the author's permission.

Excerpts from *The Seven Storey Mountain* by Thomas Merton. Copyright © 1948 by Harcourt Brace & Company and renewed 1976 by the Trustees of The Merton Legacy Trust. Reprinted by permission of the publisher. English-language rights outside the U.S.

Index

Abbey of Gethsemani, 16, 134-35, 149, 191-92. *See also* Dom Flavian; Dom Frederic; Dom James; Trappists
Alaska, 178-79

Baez, Joan, 117
Bamberger, John Eudes, 107, 131
Barber, John, 3, 49
Bennett, Tom: 9, 46, 53; Tom and Iris, 59-60, 70-71, 72-73
Bermuda, 20-22
Berrigan, Daniel, 173
Blake, William, 56-57, 81
Bramachari, 79
Burns, Flavian. *See* Dom Flavian

Burton, Naomi, 129, 130, 146

Camaldolese order, 151
Cambridge University, 2, 62, 69
Cameron, J. M., 173
Cardenal, Ernesto, 165-66
Carthusians, 151
Catholic Worker, The, 163-64
Censorship, 135, 161, 162-63, 164
Cistercians of the Strict Observance. *See* Trappists
Cold War, 158-59
Columbia University, 2, 74-77, 81, 83
Communists, 164-65, 187-88

203

Cuba, 89-90

Dalai Lama, 181-82, 183-84
Day, Dorothy, 163-64
Doherty, F. C., 54-55
Dom Flavian, 175-76, 189-90, 191
Dom Frederic, 5, 118-19, 123, 126, 130, 132-33, 136-37
Dom James, 137, 139, 148-50, 151-52, 153, 166-67, 173, 174
Douglaston, N.Y., 10, 14, 17, 19, 26-27

Ferlinghetti, Lawrence, 176, 179
Ferry, W. H., 179, 190
Flood, Maurice, 192
Forest, James, 164
Fox, James. *See* Dom James
Franciscans, 88-89, 91-93
Freedgood, Seymour, 76, 79, 90-91

Gerdy, Bob, 76, 79, 90
Gibney, Bob, 76, 79, 90
Gilson, Étienne, 80
Giroux, Robert, 5-6, 75-76, 79, 128, 129, 130, 138
Greene, Graham, 137

Haughton family, 47
Hopkins, Gerard Manley, 81

India, 180-82, 184-85

Jadot, Jean, 155-56
Jenkins, Harold, 68
Jenkins, Martha and Samuel, 10, 14, 17, 22-25, 33-34, 52-54, 69, 77, 119
Jerwood, Buggy, 50

Kramer, Victor, 121

Laughlin, James, 121, 123-24, 126-27, 130
Lax, Robert, 3, 6-7, 76, 79, 90, 117, 120-21
Leclercq, Jean, 175
Luce, Clare Booth, 137-38

Marsh, Reginald, 68-69
Merton, John Paul, 11-12, 23, 33-34, 67, 85, 95, 115-17
Merton, Owen, 8-11, 13-14, 30-31; as artist, 10-11, 21-22, 27, 32-33, 40; death of, 56; illness of, 25-26, 46-47, 48-49, 53-54, 55; as parent, 19, 20-21, 29,

204

40; travels of, 8, 17, 18, 41-42

Merton, Ruth (née Jenkins), 9-15, 17

Merton, Thomas: baptism, 2, 9, 82; birth of, 8; and censorship of writing, 135, 161, 162-63, 164; controversial views of, 160-66; death of, 188-92; and decision to join Trappist order, 3-4, 83-105; and ecumenism, 175, 180-81, 186-88; and fame, 139, 151, 160, 162-63; father's influence on, 32-33, 123; and hermitage, 167-71; and human rights, 161-62; and interest in Eastern religions, 154-56, 160-61, 172-74, 182-84, 185-86; journals of, 145-47; and love of nature, 154, 168-72; and Marxism, 187-88; as Master of Novices, 152-53, 165-66, 171; as Master of Scholastics, 147-48; as novice at Gethsemani, 109-20; and ordination as Trappist, 1, 5-7, 141; on peace and war, 163-64; as postulant at Gethsemani, 106-9; religious development of, 2-3, 9, 13-14, 25, 29, 31, 41, 45, 63-65, 66-82, 97-100, 102; schooling of, 2, 12-13, 17-18, 20-21, 31, 34-37, 43-45, 49-51, 54-55, 61; and social issues, 85-86, 100-101, 159-62; and solitude, 112-13, 132, 150, 167-71; and taking of solemn vows, 133-34; and thoughts about leaving order, 130-31, 151-52, 153; and writing, 36, 43, 44, 86, 87, 112-14, 118, 119-20, 131-33, 135-36, 159

Works:

The Alaskan Journal, 146

The Ascent to Truth, 144

The Asian Journal, 146, 179

The Cold War Letters, 163

Conjectures of a Guilty Bystander, 146, 159

Elected Silence, 139

Exile Ends in Glory, 135

Figures for an Apocalypse, 135

"For My Brother Reported Missing in Action, 1943," 117

Gandhi on Non-Violence, 172

"The Labyrinth," 86, 94

A Man in the Divided Sea, 122, 123

"The Man in the Sycamore Tree," 86

My Argument with the Gestapo, 36

Mystics and Zen Masters, 172

New Seeds of Contemplation, 145

Peace in the Post-Christian Era, 164

The Secular Journal (The Cuban Journal), 146

Seeds of Contemplation, 144, 145

Seeds of Destruction, 159

The Seven Storey Mountain, 126-30, 135, 136, 137-39, 147

The Sign of Jonas, 146

The Tears of the Blind Lions, 144

Thirty Poems, 120-22, 123

A Vow of Conversation, 146, 168

The Waters of Siloe, 135, 144

The Way of Chuang Tzu, 172

What Are These Wounds? 145

Woods, Shore, Desert, 146, 177

Zen and the Birds of Appetite, 172

Montauban, France, 28-29

Murat, France, 38

Our Lady of the Redwoods, 176, 179

Pearce, Benjamin and Maud, 42-44, 53, 69

Philotheus (Father), 102, 103

Prades, France, 8-9

Privat, Monsieur and Madame, 38-40, 41

Provincetown, Mass., 18-19

Reinhardt, Ad, 90

Rice, Ed, 76, 79, 90, 91, 139, 173

Rome, Italy, 63

St. Antonin, France, 30-32, 40

Seven Mountains of Thomas Merton, The, 35-36

Sri Lanka (Ceylon), 185-86

Suzuki, D. T., 155, 173

Thailand, 180, 186-88

Tibet, 183-84

Tobin, Mary Luke, 160-61, 164

Trappists, 4, 95-96, 100, 107, 110-11. *See also* Abbey of Gethsemani;

Dom Flavian; Dom Frederic; Dom James

Trier, Gwyneth, 53

Van Doren, Mark, 74, 79, 102, 104, 121

Vietnam War, 187, 191

Wakefield, Norma, 58

Walsh, Dan, 83, 87, 88, 95

Waugh, Evelyn, 137

Wilkes, Paul, 49

Winser, Andrew, 72

World War II, 85, 91-92, 94-95